Current
CONTROVERSIES

Conserving the Environment

Other Books in the Current Controversies series

Conserving
the Environment

Debra A. Miller, Book Editor

GREENHAVEN PRESS
A part of Gale, Cengage Learning

GALE
CENGAGE Learning·

Detroit • New York • San Francisco • New Haven, Conn • Waterville, Maine • London

Christine Nasso, *Publisher*
Elizabeth Des Chenes, *Managing Editor*

© 2010 Greenhaven Press, a part of Gale, Cengage Learning

Gale and Greenhaven Press are registered trademarks used herein under license.

For more information, contact:
Greenhaven Press
27500 Drake Rd.
Farmington Hills, MI 48331-3535
Or you can visit our Internet site at gale.cengage.com

For product information and technology assistance, contact us at

Gale Customer Support, 1-800-877-4253
For permission to use material from this text or product, submit all requests online at www.cengage.com/permissions

Further permissions questions can be emailed to permissionrequest@cengage.com

Articles in Greenhaven Press anthologies are often edited for length to meet page requirements. In addition, original titles of these works are changed to clearly present the main thesis and to explicitly indicate the author's opinion. Every effort is made to ensure that Greenhaven Press accurately reflects the original intent of the authors. Every effort has been made to trace the owners of copyrighted material.

Cover image © Specialist Stock/Encyclopedia/Corbis.

LIBRARY OF CONGRESS CATALOGING-IN-PUBLICATION DATA

Conserving the environment / Debra A. Miller, book editor.
    p. cm. -- (Current controversies)
    Includes bibliographical references and index.
    ISBN 978-0-7377-4661-7 (hbk.) -- ISBN 978-0-7377-4662-4 (pbk.)
    1. Environmental protection--Juvenile literature. 2. Global warming--Juvenile literature. 3. Environmentalism--Juvenile literature. I. Miller, Debra A.
    TD170.15.C67 2010
    363.7--dc22
                                                            2009037782

Printed in the United States of America
2 3 4 5 6   16 15 14 13 12

FD018

Contents

Chapter 1: How Serious Is the Global Environmental Crisis?

Chapter 2: Is Global Warming a Real Threat?

Yes: Global Warming Is a Real Threat

Chapter 3: Is Biodiversity Loss a Major Concern?

Chapter 4: What Steps Are Necessary to Better Protect the Environment?

Foreword

By definition, controversies are "discussions of questions in which opposing opinions clash" (*Webster's Twentieth Century Dictionary Unabridged*). Few would deny that controversies are a pervasive part of the human condition and exist on virtually every level of human enterprise. Controversies transpire between individuals and among groups, within nations and between nations. Controversies supply the grist necessary for progress by providing challenges and challengers to the status quo. They also create atmospheres where strife and warfare can flourish. A world without controversies would be a peaceful world; but it also would be, by and large, static and prosaic.

The Series' Purpose

The purpose of the *Current Controversies* series is to explore many of the social, political, and economic controversies dominating the national and international scenes today. Titles selected for inclusion in the series are highly focused and specific. For example, from the larger category of criminal justice, *Current Controversies* deals with specific topics such as police brutality, gun control, white collar crime, and others. The debates in *Current Controversies* also are presented in a useful, timeless fashion. Articles and book excerpts included in each title are selected if they contribute valuable, long-range ideas to the overall debate. And wherever possible, current information is enhanced with historical documents and other relevant materials. Thus, while individual titles are current in focus, every effort is made to ensure that they will not become quickly outdated. Books in the *Current Controversies* series will remain important resources for librarians, teachers, and students for many years.

In addition to keeping the titles focused and specific, great care is taken in the editorial format of each book in the series. Book introductions and chapter prefaces are offered to provide background material for readers. Chapters are organized around several key questions that are answered with diverse opinions representing all points on the political spectrum. Materials in each chapter include opinions in which authors clearly disagree as well as alternative opinions in which authors may agree on a broader issue but disagree on the possible solutions. In this way, the content of each volume in *Current Controversies* mirrors the mosaic of opinions encountered in society. Readers will quickly realize that there are many viable answers to these complex issues. By questioning each author's conclusions, students and casual readers can begin to develop the critical thinking skills so important to evaluating opinionated material.

Current Controversies is also ideal for controlled research. Each anthology in the series is composed of primary sources taken from a wide gamut of informational categories including periodicals, newspapers, books, U.S. and foreign government documents, and the publications of private and public organizations. Readers will find factual support for reports, debates, and research papers covering all areas of important issues. In addition, an annotated table of contents, an index, a book and periodical bibliography, and a list of organizations to contact are included in each book to expedite further research.

Perhaps more than ever before in history, people are confronted with diverse and contradictory information. During the Persian Gulf War, for example, the public was not only treated to minute-to-minute coverage of the war, it was also inundated with critiques of the coverage and countless analyses of the factors motivating U.S. involvement. Being able to sort through the plethora of opinions accompanying today's major issues, and to draw one's own conclusions, can be a complicated and frustrating struggle. It is the editors' hope that *Current Controversies* will help readers with this struggle.

Introduction

> *"International concern about the environment is a fairly recent phenomenon . . . and it has yet to reverse what many scientists say is a rapid degradation of the planet's rich resources and ecosystems."*

The concept of environmental sustainability—basically the idea that humans should live on the Earth without damaging the environment for future generations—is commonly invoked these days as the goal that must be achieved by all peoples and all nations in order to preserve the health of the global environment. But this international concern about the environment is a fairly recent phenomenon, rooted in an American environmental movement that arose in the 1960s and 1970s, and it has yet to reverse what many scientists say is a rapid degradation of the planet's rich resources and ecosystems.

The global environmental movement is based on earlier environmental efforts in the United States. This American environmental movement began with the publishing of a book called *A Silent Spring* in 1962. Authored by marine biologist Rachel Carson, the book described the health and environmental hazards of the pesticide DDT, which was widely used at that time in the United States and around the world. Carson's writing caused many Americans to realize that industrialization and economic development had exploited and damaged the natural environment, and this realization helped to launch an environmental movement dedicated to regulating industry in order to protect environmental resources. Over the next few decades, environmental advocacy groups were formed; annual Earth Day events were held to publicize environmental issues; and the U.S. government created the Environmental Protection Agency to begin addressing problems of pollution and environmental damage. A number of other developed countries followed a similar path of growing environmental awareness.

Many commentators claim that the American-inspired environmental movement lost its way during the 1980s due to the election of leaders such as President Ronald Reagan, whose policies were decidedly anti-environmental and pro-business. And as poorer countries began to develop, most of them following the same environmentally damaging path used by the United States and other highly industrialized nations, environmental problems became more globalized. Faced with problems such as widespread deforestation and climate changes, people began to see that environmental damage in one part of the world can also harm other parts of the world. Increasingly, environmentalists focused not only on regulating industries that pollute, but also on making all human development activities—including manufacturing, agriculture, energy production, transportation, and homebuilding—environmentally sustainable over the long term.

This "sustainable development" concept was first popularized in 1987 when the World Commission on Environment and Development, a United Nations (UN) commission created to address global environmental problems, issued a report, titled *Our Common Future*. The report, commonly known as "The Bruntland Report," explained that the commission was asked to formulate "long-term environmental strategies for achieving sustainable development by the year 2000 and beyond." It defined environmental sustainability as "meeting the needs of the present without compromising the ability of future generations to meet their own needs." The report's main message was that the Earth's environment is shared by all people and that the economic development paths of all nations must become sustainable in order for the planet's hospitality and future generations of humans to survive.

The Bruntland Report helped to launch what has now become an international environmental movement focused on achieving sustainability. The movement began in 1992 with a UN Conference on Environment and Development in Rio de Janeiro, Brazil. Later that year, the UN established a separate division called the Commission on Sustainable Development. In 1997, the UN sponsored the Kyoto Conference on Global Warming—a meeting that led to the Kyoto Protocol, which set specific targets for industrialized nations to reduce greenhouse gas emissions believed to be contributing to climate change.

In September 2000, building on this history of international concern for the environment and development, members of the UN adopted the United Nations Millennium Declaration, which created a new global partnership aimed at reducing extreme poverty and promoting sustainable development. The declaration set out a series of goals, called the Millennium Development Goals, with a deadline of 2015. One of those goals, Goal #7, stated:

> Reducing poverty and achieving sustained development must be done in conjunction with a healthy planet. The Millennium Goals recognize that environmental sustainability is part of global economic and social well-being. Unfortunately exploitation of natural resources such as forests, land, water, and fisheries—often by the powerful few—have caused alarming changes in our natural world in recent decades, often harming the most vulnerable people in the world who depend on natural resources for their livelihood.

To remedy these global environmental problems, the UN pledged to "integrate the principles of sustainable development into country policies and programmes; reverse loss of environmental resources; reduce by half the proportion of people without sustainable access to safe drinking water; and achieve significant improvement in lives of at least 100 million slum dwellers by 2020."

The international interest in sustainability suggests that people around the world are finally beginning to realize that we all live on the same planet, breathe the same air, and depend on the same recycled natural resources to survive and prosper. Unfortunately, according to most scientists and environmentalists, the environmental effort has so far failed to stop or slow down the ongoing process of environmental deterioration occurring around the planet. Scientists continue to warn of serious environmental problems—such as global warming, threats to the Earth's ozone layer, the loss of agricultural land, the drying up of rivers and aquifers, and losses of plant and animal biodiversity—that could threaten the very survival of human civilization in future decades.

The UN's 2008 *Millennium Development Goals Report*, for example, found that only limited progress had been made to fulfill the goals of encouraging sustainable development, stopping biodiversity loss, improving water resources, and eradicating poverty. The report urged that immediate action be taken to contain rising greenhouse gas emissions linked to global warming, to conserve marine and forest areas that are vulnerable to biodiversity losses, and to protect fish and other plant and animal species threatened with extinction. The report also stressed the urgent need to slow the depletion of the world's water supplies and provide the poor with safe drinking water and sanitation facilities.

Achieving a consensus to tackle these huge environmental problems appears to be the challenge of today's generation. To some extent, changes in attitude seem to be happening at a rapid rate; even industry seems to be realizing that economic well-being is dependent on a healthy environment. Wal-Mart, for example, adopted a sustainability program in 2005 that committed the company to changing its business practices—everything from the materials used to build its stores to the items stocked on its shelves—to "green" choices. At the same time, however, there continue to be vocal critics who dispute the claim that global warming is attributable to human activities and who assert that business and other human goals must take precedence over protecting the environment. The viewpoints in *Current Controversies: Conserving the Environment* describe some of the most serious environmental threats, reflect the debates regarding issues such as global warming and biodiversity, and suggest some ideas for better protecting the global environment in the future.

CHAPTER 1

How Serious Is the Global Environmental Crisis?

Chapter Preface

According to environmentalists, one of the serious problems affecting the global environment is a growing amount of human garbage, much of which contains toxic chemicals, heavy metals, or radioactive materials that are hazardous to human health and damaging for natural ecosystems. In developing countries, some garbage is recycled or otherwise regulated and safely disposed of, but the majority of rich nations' trash ends up in gigantic landfills. These modern landfills are lined and vented to try to contain noxious fumes and toxins and prevent them from escaping into the nearby environment; yet environmentalists argue that even the best landfill lining will someday deteriorate. The garbage situation in less developed parts of the world is much less regulated. In poorer countries, mountains of trash often build up on residential streets and in open-air dumps, raising alarming health, safety, and environmental issues. Some developing countries have even begun to import trash from richer nations, adding to their garbage problems. Garbage is even accumulating in the vast Pacific Ocean, where a soup of non-biodegradable plastic materials covers an area twice the size of the continental United States.

Modern trash includes not only organic biodegradable trash (such as food scraps and paper products) and non-biodegradable materials (such as plastics), but also truly hazardous substances. And this hazardous waste can be anything from small amounts of poisonous household products to large quantities of highly toxic industrial chemicals. Some of the most dangerous types of wastes are radioactive nuclear wastes; chemical pesticides, herbicides, and fertilizers; and E-waste—products such as old computers, cell phones, and other electronics. Some countries, such as the United States, require most hazardous wastes to be cleaned up and disposed of in ways that minimize dangers to the public and the environment, but in many less developed parts of the world these dangerous materials remain wholly unregulated.

Hazardous industrial wastes—such as toxic chemicals, solvents, pesticides, and heavy metals—pose some of the greatest threats to the environment. Industrial manufacturing operations in developed nations around the world have produced large quantities of hazardous wastes for the past 100 years, and before they were regulated, most of these wastes were simply allowed to vent into the atmosphere or were dumped into waterways or into the ground. The danger of hazardous industrial wastes to human health and the environment has been repeatedly shown in environmental disasters around the world. One such event occurred in the 1970s at Love Canal, an industrial dump site in the city of Niagara Falls, New York. A chemical company had dumped 21,000 tons of chemicals into the area for a period of thirty-three years, and these toxins, many of them now known to be potent carcinogens, eventually began sickening the local population. Another industrial disaster took place at a Union Carbide pesticide plant in the city of Bhopal, India. On December 3, 1984, the plant released 42 tons of toxic methyl isocyanate gas into the atmosphere, killing thousands of nearby residents. The Bhopal incident is often called the world's worst industrial disaster.

Agricultural activities are another way in which hazardous wastes enter the environment. Enormous amounts of hazardous chemical pesticides and herbicides are used on crops by agriculture producers each year, and many of these chemicals run off as pollution into the soil and groundwater. In addition, many farmers use fertilizers made from recycled industrial hazardous wastes. These materials contain nutrients, such as nitrogen, phosphorus, and potassium, that are beneficial to plants, but they also contain toxins such as mercury, lead, cadmium, arsenic, uranium, nickel, chromium, and dioxins that can contaminate large stretches of valuable topsoil. Another fertilizer source is sewage sludge, which may contain dangerous levels of pathogens, as well as polychlorinated biphenyls (toxic organic fluids known as PCBs), chlorinated pesticides, asbestos, industrial solvents, petroleum products, radioactive material, and heavy metals.

In addition, rapid advances in technology in the past few decades have created a new hazardous waste problem in the form of E-waste. Some have estimated that up to 400 million tons of E-waste are generated each year worldwide. This waste, made up of computers, TVs, cell phones, and other electronic items, can contain a host of hazardous materials such as chlorinated solvents, brominated flame retardants, PVC (a thermoplastic resin), heavy metals, plastics, and gases. Much of this E-waste is produced by rich nations but exported to developing countries, where the absence of government regulations often exposes poor workers to health hazards. The hazardous E-waste stream is expected to explode to even greater proportions in the future, as technology continues its relentless advance and as developing nations add billions of new electronics consumers to the world market.

Some of the most dangerous hazardous wastes, however, are high-level radioactive nuclear wastes produced when uranium is mined for use as nuclear fuel, or later when nuclear power plants produce spent fuel that is highly radioactive. Mining, for example, creates radioactive tailings that can pollute waterways or drift into the air and can persist in the environment for up to 100,000 years. Many uranium mining sites, have become environmental wastelands, unfit for human habitation. Nuclear reactors, used to produce electricity, also create tons of dangerous radioactive material that slowly decays for thousands of years. These nuclear wastes pose one of the most difficult problems because no one has found a viable, permanent disposal solution for wastes that stay radioactive virtually forever. Most countries that operate nuclear reactors either store it in containers on the Earth's surface, bury it into the ground in containers, or reprocess it into solid glass or ceramic blocks for deep burial.

Opinions differ as to the severity of the hazardous garbage threat for the global environment. The authors of the viewpoints in this chapter lay out some of the other serious environmental challenges in our modern world.

Climate Change Is a Serious Problem

Current Events

Current Events is an educational magazine which contains in-depth coverage of national and world news presented in a student-friendly format for those in grades 1-10.

Devastating wildfires rage in California. In Bangladesh, massive floods wipe out coastal villages. Frogs are vanishing from the Costa Rican rain forest. In the Arctic, polar bears are drowning.

At first glance, those very different catastrophes seem to have little in common. A new report compiled by scientists from around the world, however, suggests they are all the result of global climate change.

In April [2007], the United Nations' Intergovernmental Panel on Climate Change (IPCC) released a report on global warming. In it, scientists make some dire predictions about how climate changes will affect life.

Predicting the Affects of Climate Change

By 2080, scientists estimate, the number of people going hungry in the world could increase by between 140 million and 1 billion, depending on the amount of greenhouse gases emitted over the coming years. Outbreaks of diseases such as dengue fever, malaria, and diarrhea, plus heat–related deaths, are likely to increase dramatically. By 2020, up to 250 million people could face water shortages in Africa. If average temperatures rise by 2.7 to 4.5 degrees Fahrenheit, about 20 to 50 percent of plant and animal species face increased risk of extinction.

Poor people will be hit the hardest. "It's the poorest of the poor in the world, and this includes the poor people even in prosperous societies, who are going to be the worst hit," says Rajendra Pachauri, IPCC chairperson.

Wealthy nations such as the United States are equally vulnerable to climate change. Scientists predict that melting glaciers and warming temperatures are very likely to reduce water supplies in the western United States. The East Coast, meanwhile, is likely to see rising water levels and an increase in storm surges that could flood both New York City and Boston.

To some scientists, the report sounds alarmist. But IPCC scientists say they based their predictions not simply on theoretical models but on hard data. Many of the trends they foresee, they say, have already begun.

Rising Temperatures

For years, climate change has been the subject of heated debate. However; most scientists now agree that, since 1750, temperatures have been steadily rising. Eleven of the past 12 years have been the warmest on record. "Warming of the climate system is unequivocal, as is now evident from observations of increases in global average air and ocean temperatures, widespread melting of snow and ice, and rising global average sea level," the IPCC stated in a February report.

The Cause and Solution of Global Warming

The IPCC's February report made headlines because it stated, with 90 percent certainty, that human activity is responsible for global warming. Carbon dioxide, methane, and nitrous oxide trap heat in Earth's atmosphere, causing the greenhouse effect. The report says the increase in carbon dioxide in Earth's atmosphere comes from burning fossil fuels such as coal and oil. Increases in methane and nitrous oxide emissions are primarily attributed to agriculture.

If human activity is causing the problem, can people take action to solve it? Yes, says Achim Steiner. He is executive director of the U.N. Environment Programme, one of two U.N. agencies that sponsored the panel. Steiner says the best way to reduce global warming is to make "deep and decisive cuts in greenhouse gas emissions." Although many countries have set limits on such emissions, the United States, which produces the highest levels of greenhouse gases, has not. Carbon dioxide emissions are regulated mostly at the state level rather than at the federal level.

In March, former Vice President Al Gore testified before Congress about the need to act. He urged lawmakers to cap carbon dioxide emissions. "We do not have time to play around with this," Gore said. "Our world faces a true planetary emergency."

In his 2007 State of the Union address, U.S. President George W. Bush acknowledged the "serious challenge" presented by global climate change. So far, however, the Bush administration has rejected calls to limit carbon dioxide emissions. The Bush administration says that mandating lower emissions would hurt the U.S. economy. Texas Rep. Joseph Barton, the leading Republican on the House Energy and Commerce Committee, agrees. Barton also questions whether limiting emissions would have any effect, calling the science of global warming "uneven and evolving."

Barton's statements, however; seem to represent the minority viewpoint these days. "The science now is getting to the point where it's pretty hard to deny," Christine Todd Whitman, former head of the U.S. Environmental Protection Agency under George W. Bush, told *Time* magazine. Even so, finding solutions that everyone can agree on promises to be the biggest challenge.

Study Observations

The Intergovernmental Panel on Climate Change based its report released in April on data and studies dating to 1970.

Many of the studies observed the physical and biological environment and their relationships to climate changes. The report included more than 29,000 observational data series from 75 studies. The studies tracked everything from how recent warming has affected the timing of spring events such as bird migration, egg laying, and leaf unfolding to how warmer water affected fish migration, plankton, and algae. More than 89 percent of the data showed changes that were consistent with what would be expected in response to global warning.

The report notes a lack of geographical balance in the studies and scarcity of data in developing countries. That is noteworthy, because people in developing countries are most vulnerable to the effects of climate change.

Climate Change Is Not a Catastrophe

Kevin Berger

Kevin Berger is the features editor at Salon, *an online magazine.*

Bjørn Lomborg drives people crazy. The tale of the controversy that swarmed his 2001 book, *The Skeptical Environmentalist*, in which the native Dane argued that many environmental problems were overblown, has been widely told. With a few clicks you can read all about his skirmish with the Danish Committees on Scientific Dishonesty and his protracted battle with *Scientific American*. In a flash you can find his defenders strafing his critics from their libertarian bunkers or congressional offices. When Sen. James Inhofe, R-Okla., wants to back up his claim that global warming is the "greatest hoax ever perpetrated on the American people," or invites somebody to Washington to debate Al Gore, he calls on Lomborg.

Lomborg, 42, rose to infamy by way of a Ph.D. in political science and a love affair with statistics. Today he is an adjunct professor at the Copenhagen Business School and the director of the Copenhagen Concensus Center, where he strives to devise economic solutions to the world's pressing problems. Next week he will storm back into the cultural fray with *Cool It: The Skeptical Environmentalist's Guide to Global Warming*, a highly readable asseveration that global warming is not so bad and that Al Gore is an inconvenient truth-stretcher. . . .

Kevin Berger: Why did you write Cool It?

Bjørn Lomborg: Because we're stuck in this unproductive question, Is global warming a hoax or a catastrophe? Left-wingers say it's a catastrophe and we need to change our entire means of production and society. Right-wingers say we shouldn't bother with it all. If they were right, those conclusions might follow, but that's not what the science tells us. The science tells us that global warming is a problem but not a catastrophe. On the other hand, it's not a hoax. I'm trying to make a middle ground for arguing that this is not a problem that will be solved within the next five or 10 years. This is a problem that will take a half or full century, and we need to be sure we have good ways of dealing with it.

You write, "Doing too little about climate change is definitely wrong. But so is doing too much." Why?

Doing too little is obvious, but let's say it anyway: If you don't do something about global warming, of course it will become a bigger problem. So obviously we need to address it and in the long term fix it. On the other hand, doing too much about it means we are focusing too much effort on climate change and forgetting all the other things that we have a responsibility to deal with, like HIV/AIDS, tuberculosis, malaria and malnutrition. If we spend too much time and resources focusing on climate change, then we do the future a disservice because we say, "Hey, we fixed climate change but we let all the other things slide."

People will have to deal with more climate change, but maybe overall they'll be better off.

How can you separate climate change, which would lead to the despoilation of all the earth's living systems, from those problems? They are interrelated. What good does it do to treat them as separate?

It's clear that they are all interrelated. But one of the things that seems curious in the climate change discussion is the insistence that climate change is linked to all these other issues. But they are equally linked back. When we talk about how global warming is going to make people more vulnerable to malaria, that's absolutely true. At the same time, rampant malaria is going to make everyone much more vulnerable to climate change. In a perfect world, we should fix all problems. But in a world where we haven't fixed all the problems in the last 50 years, it makes sense to ask, If you fix a large chunk of malaria, how much good do you do?

Yes, people will have to deal with more climate change, but maybe overall they'll be better off. It's like when your family has to decide where to live. It would be nice to have a great house and be close to a good school. But there's also a budget restriction. So you make trade-offs and say some things are more important to focus on first.

The best investment we can do is prevention of HIV/ AIDS. For every dollar you spend on prevention of HIV/ AIDS, you'll end up doing $40 worth of good.

Why do you assume there is a zero sum of money for the world's problems and that it has to [be] partitioned for one thing and not the other?

So you're saying, What if we had $1 billion for malaria and $1 billion for climate? Why not do both?

Isn't that how the world works? There are a lot of organizations devoted to these problems. The Bill and Melinda Gates Foundation gives billions to help fight malaria and AIDS. One organization or government doesn't steal from the other, right?

Recently the Global Fund to Fight AIDS, Tuberculosis and Malaria came out and said we have to recognize that over the coming years, because of the incredible attention to climate change, we're probably going to get much less money. [The Global Fund "is not naive about what (the increased importance of) global warming will do to AIDs funding in a few years' time," said John Linden, head of communications, as reported in the *Financial Times*.]

My point is much simpler. Let's assume we had $1 billion for each of these areas. If the $1 billion in malaria does a lot more good than the $1 billion in climate, and assuming that the next $1 billion will do the same thing, I would still argue, shouldn't we then have a conversation about perhaps spending both billions on malaria and none on climate change? I'm not saying that's what we should do. But I'm saying we need to have that conversation. If we could spend that money better somewhere else, shouldn't we? . . .

Tell us a little more about the Copenhagen Consensus.

We assembled a panel of eminent experts, including four Nobel laureates, to look at all these different problem areas and say, "Yeah, I know you think your solution is good, but we have to compare it to everyone else's." They asked, How much good can we do for every dollar spent? And ranked all the opportunities. It turned out that the best investment we can do is prevention of HIV/AIDS. For every dollar you spend on prevention of HIV/AIDS, you'll end up doing $40 worth of good. The same is true with malnutrition. For every dollar you spend on micronutrients, basically a vitamin pill, you would do about $30 worth of good. And that would affect more than half the world's population. With malaria, for every dollar you spend on mosquito nets and information and some medicine, you'd do about $10 worth of good.

The solutions that are proposed right now to climate change are fairly poor.

Climate change ended up at the bottom of your list. So are you saying that climate change is not as significant as malaria, AIDS and malnutrition, and therefore we shouldn't spend public resources on it now?

I'm sure some people would see it that way. But what we're saying is for every $1 you spend as part of the Kyoto Protocol to reduce carbon emissions, you will do only about

30 cents' worth of good for the world. What that tells us is that the solutions that are proposed right now to climate change are fairly poor.

Malaria and AIDS are problems happening right now. How can you compare them to climate change, which will be at its most severe in the future?

In principle, we tried to value all of the impacts that these problems will have in the coming years and into the future. But we don't typically have models for malaria and HIV/AIDS like we do for global warming. So, yes, we don't know what exactly will happen to them in 2100. At the same time, we know HIV/AIDS kills a lot of people now and maims society because it takes away the primary caregivers. If we did something about it, it wouldn't just mean that people would stop dying now. It would also mean they would get much richer and be more resilient toward the end of the century to climate change. So it's not just about the people now. It would have huge effects for generations to come.

Couldn't we say that climate change is a far worse problem than malaria or AIDS or malnutrition? The resultant rise in sea level and heat, as well as the loss of biodiversity, could harm the entire planet and all species, right? Shouldn't we start solving the worst problem now?

Kyoto is both impossibly ambitious and environmentally inconsequential. It's not smart.

And the worst problem being that everyone dies on the planet? Do we then search for immortality? I'm not just being facetious. You wouldn't do that, because a search wouldn't be very valuable, right? We would not find anything, but we would spend all of our resources looking for the philosopher's stone. It just doesn't make sense to talk about what's the problem without thinking about what's the solution. As for your idea that this could spoil the entire earth and so it's a much bigger problem than malaria, well, again, climate change is a problem, but it's not a catastrophe. It's not the end of the world by any means.

[The] primary solution is to focus on research and development.

At the end of the day, Kyoto is both impossibly ambitious and environmentally inconsequential. It's not smart. It's just not in the nature of the political process to say we're going to do something now to solve a problem later on. So instead of saying, "Let's do something that feels good right now," let's try and think of what we could do that will *do* good now.

Which is what?

My primary solution is to focus on research and development. Invest .05 percent of GDP, or $25 billion, in the R&D of energy technologies that don't emit carbon. The problem now is we focus on cutting emissions. Basically we're going to spend almost all of the money to meet Kyoto on buying windmills or solar cells or, more likely, natural gas instead of coal, or more expensive ways of doing production. It seems reasonable for me to ask, Does that do very much good?

I agree that when you make it more expensive to use fossil fuels, people will spend more money on research and development. But let's not buy things right now that make us feel good but result in fairly trivial carbon cuts. As you probably know, we have lots of windmills in Denmark. We felt incredibly good about this in the '80s and '90s. So we spent a lot on windmills that turned out to [be] inefficient. Now we basically have to take down all our old windmills and put up the new efficient ones. My point is that maybe we shouldn't have put up the first ones. We should have invested in research and development and waited to put up bigger, better windmills.

But wasn't that a necessary process? Creating the first windmills is what led to the development of better ones.

Yes, but if you want to get a better windmill, maybe you put up one or 10 or even 100. Economists disagree on this. But you don't need 1,000 or 10,000. My point is: Don't do stuff before it's efficient, but make sure you get faster to the point where it gets efficient.

[We] should spend $25 billion on climate change but not $180 billion—which is how much it would cost . . . [to reduce] carbon emissions below 1990 levels.

But if we refocus our political energy away from climate change to the other problems you mention, aren't we then putting a barrier in front of the kind of research and development that you want? Isn't that dangerous?

But if you grant that argument, I would also say if we focus attention away from HIV/AIDS and malaria and malnutrition, that would also seem dangerous. That's why we need to have a sense of balance. I'm saying you should spend $25 billion on climate change but not $180 billion—which is how much it would cost each year if the U.S. and everybody else lived up to the Kyoto protocol of reducing carbon emissions below 1990 levels. The $180 billion is the average outcome of all macroeconomic models gathered by the Stanford economic energy modeling forum.

All macroeconomic models?

Obviously not all. But it's all the main academic models from the very optimistic, which say it's only going to cost $50 billion, to the very pessimistic ones, which the Bush government likes to use, that show it's going to cost $400 billion. It's basically saying, "Don't take the most optimistic, and don't take the most pessimistic either. But take the average of that." This is not a true number. But it's in that range.

Should global priorities really be set by a cost-benefit analysis?

Oh, God, no. Not at all. We are saying the Copenhagen Consensus is the price list. Essentially we're providing the prices on the social menu of what you can choose to do. No, no, no. Economists don't set the agenda of the world. Hopefully democracies do. You and I. So it's nice to know how much will this cost, how much good will this do. If you go into a restaurant and say, "The only thing I'm going to buy is beluga caviar," that's fine, that's your choice, but at least now you know what the prices are.

I don't know, Bjørn, cost-benefit analysis seems to be how we got into this trouble in the first place. The oil and automobile companies, for instance, determined that we can pump out this much pollution because it will amount to this much profit, and that's a viable trade-off.

Obviously it's a very different thing when private companies make that choice. Private companies don't care if somebody else has to pay [for] the pollution, and that makes sense.

Shouldn't private companies have a social responsibility?

Well, maybe. If you were a CEO and you had your responsibility to the stockholders, I think it's unreasonable to expect that they would have a huge amount of extra social responsibility. That's what societies have to regulate. That's why we have to make taxes, make environmental regulations, set boundaries, say, "No, you can't do that" or, "Yes, you can do that." Clearly you have to regulate that.

Our job here is to fix the most important things, ... so that we leave the best possible future for our kids. But they'll also have to fend for themselves on some of the problems.

So I would say it's not that way of thinking that's gotten us into trouble. Think back 150 years, when we really started churning out a lot of CO_2, and started using coal and then later oil in a massive fashion. If you had been back there then and known about all these problems, how much would you have changed? My sense is you would have said, "I want my kids and grandkids to be well off. I want them to be without diseases. I want them to have a good education and good nutrition." So a lot of good things happened because of fossil fuels. We're now starting to realize that wasn't the case, and we will have to start dealing with it.

But we constantly make trade-offs and ask, To what extent are we willing to let something be a future generation's problem? If we are rational, then we do try to make rational cost-benefit analyses. I'm not saying we must leave some problems for future generations. But it's important to say that we always have. We have never fixed all problems. It's never been like a generation handed over a clean slate and said, "Everything is fixed." Our job here is to fix the most important things, the ones where we can do the most impact, so that we leave the best possible future for our kids. But they'll also have to fend for themselves on some of the problems.

Increasing Air Pollution Is Creating Atmospheric Brown Clouds

United Nations Environment Programme

This report was compiled by multiple authors for the United Nations Environment Programme, which is an international organization that coordinates the United Nations' environmental acitivities.

Increasing amount[s] of soot, sulphates and other aerosol components in atmospheric brown clouds (ABCs) are causing major threats to the water and food security of Asia and have resulted in surface dimming, atmospheric solar heating and soot deposition in the Hindu Kush-Himalayan-Tibetan (HKHT) glaciers and snow packs. These have given rise to major areas of concern, some of the most critical being observed decreases in the Indian summer monsoon rainfall, a north-south shift in rainfall patterns in eastern China, the accelerated retreat of the HKHT glaciers and decrease in snow packs, and the increase in surface ozone. All these have led to negative effects on water resources and crop yields. The emergence of the ABC problem is expected to further aggravate the recent dramatic escalation of food prices and the consequent challenge for survival among the world's most vulnerable populations. Lastly, the human fatalities from indoor and outdoor exposures to ABC-relevant pollutants have also become a source of grave concern.

Atmospheric Brown Cloud Hotspots

ABCs start as indoor and outdoor air pollution consisting of particles and pollutant gases, such as nitrogen oxides (NO_x), carbon monoxide (CO), sulphur dioxide (SO_2), ammonia (NH_3), and hundreds of organic gases and acids. Widespread ABC plumes resulting from the combustion of biofuels from indoors; biomass burning outdoors and fossil fuels, are found in all densely inhabited regions and oceanic regions downwind of populated continents.

Five regional ABC hotspots around the world have been identified:

1. East Asia

2. Indo-Gangetic Plain in South Asia

3. Southeast Asia

4. Southern Africa; and

5. the Amazon Basin. . . .

Substantial loadings of ABCs over Eastern USA and Europe have also been observed. However, in these extra-tropical regions, the atmospheric concentrations of ABCs are large mainly during the summer season since precipitation removes the aerosols efficiently during other seasons. Furthermore, the soot concentrations are lower and hence these extra tropical regions are not included in the hotspots category. In Asia, new aircraft and satellite data have revealed that ABC plumes, measuring 1–3 km thick, surround the Hindu Kush-Himalayan-Tibetan glaciers, both from the South Asian and the East Asian sides. Between 1950 and 2002, soot emissions increased three-fold in India and five-fold in China, while sulphur emissions have increased ten-fold in China and seven-fold in India.

ABCs Radiative Forcing

The absorption of solar radiation by the surface and the atmosphere is the fundamental driver for the physical climate system, the biogeochemical cycles, and for all life on the planet. ABCs have significantly altered this radiative forcing over Asia, as summarized below.

It is certain that ABCs have caused dimming at the surface.

It is certain that soot in ABCs has increased solar heating of the atmosphere.

It is virtually certain that India and China are dimmer (at the surface) today by at least 6 per cent, compared with the pre-industrial values. Absorbed solar radiation at the surface in China and India are [much] lower today . . . compared with the pre-industrial values.

ABC-induced dimming is considered as the major causal factor for the rainfall decrease in India and for the north to south shift of the summer monsoon in Eastern China.

It is highly likely that black carbon (BC) in ABCs has increased the vertically averaged annual mean solar absorption in the troposphere by about 15 per cent and the solar heating at elevated levels over India and China by as much as 20–50 per cent.

Rainfall over the northern half of India has decreased, while the rainfall pattern in China has shifted. The southern parts of Eastern China have been receiving more rainfall since the 1950s, while the northern parts are experiencing a negative trend. The number of rainy days for all India is also decreasing, although the frequency of intense rainfall is increasing, leading to more frequent floods. The heavily populated Indo-Gangetic Plain is especially vulnerable. Rainfall over the Indo-Gangetic Plain has decreased by about 20 per cent since the 1980s.

ABC-induced dimming is considered as the major causal factor for the rainfall decrease in India and for the north to south shift of the summer monsoon in Eastern China. However, many uncertainties in modelling regional climate remain.

Stability of the Glaciers and Snow Packs

The acceleration of the retreat of the HKHT glaciers since the 1970s, in conjunction with the decrease in the summer monsoon rainfall in the Indo-Gangetic Plain region, is a major environmental problem facing Asia, threatening both the water and the food security of South and East Asia. Glaciers and snow packs provide the head-waters for Asia's major river systems, including the Indus, the Ganges, the Brahmaputra, the Mekong and the Yangtze.

Widespread deglaciation is occurring in the HKHT region. This includes a 21 per cent decrease in the area of 466 glaciers that were studied in the Indian Himalayas. About 80 per cent of the Western Tibetan glaciers are retreating.

The receding and thinning are primarily attributed in IPCC [Intergovernmental Panel on Climate Change, a United Nations entity] reports and other studies to global warming due to increases in greenhouse gases. The present report adds that soot in ABCs is another major cause of the retreat of HKHT glaciers and snow packs. The warming of the elevated atmospheric layers due to greenhouse warming is amplified by the solar heating by soot at elevated levels and an increase in solar absorption by snow and ice contaminated by the deposition of soot. New data shown in this report reveal substantial soot concentrations in the Himalayan region even at the altitude of 5 km.

If the current rate of retreat continues unabated, these glaciers and snow packs are expected to shrink by as much as 75 per cent before the year 2050, posing grave danger to the region's water security. This potential threat should be viewed in the context of the low per-capita water availability in South and East Asia, around 2000–3000 m^3/cap/year, far less than the world average of 8549 m^3/cap/year.

Projections show that most parts of South and East Asia will suffer from water stress by 2050. Water stress occurs when the demand for water exceeds the available supply during a certain period, or when poor quality restricts its use. It should be noted that the above projections, as well as similar projections in IPCC reports, do not yet account fully for ABC effects on the monsoon and the HKHT glaciers. As a result, the actual water stress situation is expected to be much worse than the projections in the available reports.

Food Security Will Be Compromised

Throughout Asia, the annual growth rate of rice harvest has decreased from 3.5 per cent (1961–1984) to 1.3 per cent (1985–1998). Similar decreases in growth rates have occurred for wheat, maize and sorghum. Multiple stresses, such as limited availability of water and air pollution concentrations, are increasing the crops' sensitivity to climate change and reducing resilience in the agricultural sector. The negative impacts of climate change will be felt most acutely in developing countries, particularly in Asia.

Without a decrease in monsoon rainfall due to ABCs and an increase in surface warming due to GHGs [greenhouse gases], the average annual rice output for nine states studied in India during 1985–1998 would have been about 6.2 million tonnes higher [which is equal to the total annual consumption of 72 million people].

A large fraction of the aerosol particles that make up ABCs originate from emissions at the Earth's surface caused by the incomplete combustion of fossil fuels and biofuels.

In addition, elevated concentrations of ground level ozone have been found to have large effects on crop yields. Experimental evidence suggests that growing season mean ozone concentrations of 30–45 ppb [parts per billion] could see crop yield losses of 10–40 per cent for sensitive varieties of wheat, rice and legumes. A recent study translated such impacts on yield into economic losses estimating that for four key crops (wheat, rice, corn and soybean) annual losses in the region of US$5 billion may occur across Japan, the Republic of Korea, and China. These studies used dose-response relationships derived from Europe and North America, recently collated scientific evidence suggests that some important Asian grown crop cultivars may actually be more sensitive to ozone than European or North American varieties. Concern for a worsening situation in the future is highlighted by projections which suggest that the annual surface mean ozone concentrations in parts of South Asia will grow faster than anywhere else in the world and exceed 50 ppb by 2030.

The most serious health impacts of [ABCs] ... include cardiovascular and pulmonary effects leading to chronic respiratory problems, hospital admissions and deaths.

Health Is at Risk

A large fraction of the aerosol particles that make up ABCs originate from emissions at the Earth's surface caused by the incomplete combustion of fossil fuels and biofuels. Humans are exposed to these particles both indoors and outdoors. The adverse health effects of such air-borne particles have been documented in many parts of the world. Some studies have been carried out in Asia, mostly in connection with indoor cooking with biofuels, wildfires and dust storm events.

The most serious health impacts of particles associated with the ABC include cardiovascular and pulmonary effects leading to chronic respiratory problems, hospital admissions and deaths. Review of the available evidence indicates that there are likely to be very significant public health impacts from the ABC....

Using concentration-response relationships from the existing literature, it is inferred that 337,000 excess deaths per year, with a 95 per cent confidence interval of 181,000–492,000, can result due to inhalation of ABCs outdoors in India and China. This would be in addition to a WHO [World Health Organization] publication estimate of 380,700 total deaths for China and 407,100 total deaths in India from indoor air pollution attributable to solid fuel use.

The economic loss resulting from deaths due to outdoor exposure to ABC[s] . . . has been crudely estimated to be 3.6 per cent of the GDP [gross domestic product, a measure of a country's economic output] in China and 2.2 per cent in India, using mid-range mortality cost estimates. However, these numbers should be interpreted with caution at this early stage. With more research data, some of the uncertainties inherent in the health impact assessment should be reduced, leading to greater precision in the estimates.

The Health of the World's Oceans Is Rapidly Declining

Pew Environmental Group

The Pew Environmental Group is the conservation arm of the Pew Charitable Trusts, a U.S. non-governmental organization that seeks to improve public policy and educate the public.

Oceans cover 71 percent of the Earth's surface. They generate most of the oxygen in our atmosphere, detoxify and recycle much of our pollution, and absorb vast quantities of carbon dioxide, a major greenhouse gas. Oceans also play a vital role in other geochemical processes that regulate the world's climate and sustain life on Earth.

The oceans and their resources are of fundamental importance to the global economy. Over half of the world's population lives within 40 miles of the coast, a figure that is expected to increase to 75 percent by mid-century. Coastal tourism and recreation generate an estimated $463 billion each year, accounting for more than 230 million jobs worldwide. In addition, tens of millions of people depend either directly or indirectly on fishing for their livelihood. The fish they catch contribute roughly 16 percent of the animal protein consumed in the world.

Despite the critical importance of the sea to human society and the health of our environment, the world's oceans are being managed as if there were no tomorrow. The growing and, in many regions, unrestrained impact of human activity is imposing fundamental, perhaps irreversible, changes on the world's marine environment. Quite simply, the health of the oceans, once perceived as impervious to human intervention, is rapidly declining, with significant adverse consequences for

Protecting Life in the Sea, Philadelpha, PA: Pew Environment Group, The Pew Charitable Trusts, 2008. Reproduced by permission.

both people and nature. Unless we stop that decline, the livelihood of hundreds of millions of people will be at risk, as will the quality of life for billions of people worldwide.

The Causes of the Oceans' Failing Health

There are many causes of the deteriorating health of the world's oceans, including overfishing, chemical and nutrient pollution, habitat alteration, introduction of exotic species, and global climate change. Collectively, these threats imperil the rich biological diversity of life in the sea. However, the effect of destructive fishing practices overshadows them all.

Each year, global fishing fleets, now numbering over 1.3 million vessels, remove in excess of 85 million metric tons (188 billion pounds) of fish and invertebrates from the world's oceans. Many scientists believe that such a staggering amount is beyond the limits of what the marine environment can sustain. In addition, destructive fishing gear deployed by many vessels causes tremendous long-term damage to essential breeding, nursery and feeding habitat for fish and other marine life. Deep-sea bottom trawls, for example, are still used extensively throughout the world despite the havoc they wreak on the marine environment. Dragging nets the size of football fields that are weighted down by massive steel doors and often attached to heavy rollers weighing five tons or more, bottom trawls frequently crush everything in their path. This destroys the delicate structures of seamounts and deep-water corals that provide critical habitat for fish and other marine life.

Ruinous fishing methods destroy habitat and add to the problem of overfishing by killing massive amounts of fish, invertebrates, birds and marine mammals.

Similarly, boats targeting swordfish, tuna and other species leave a deadly wake. Armed with monofilament lines up to 40 miles long that are baited with hundreds or even thousands of hooks, these fishing vessels indiscriminately strip life from the sea. In addition to the species they seek, seabirds, sea turtles, sharks, whales and many undersize fish are caught and killed.

These ruinous fishing methods destroy habitat and add to the problem of overfishing by killing massive amounts of fish, invertebrates, birds and marine mammals that are inadvertently caught and thrown back, dead and dying, into the sea, a phenomenon referred to as bycatch.

The Impact on Ocean Life

The overall impact of these practices on ocean life is staggering, and has grown steadily worse over the past 50 years. Increasing numbers of boats, using more sophisticated technology, chase an ever dwindling supply of fish. In many regions of the world, there is no effective management regime to impose limits on how many fish can be taken from the sea. And even regions with a skeletal management system lack adequate enforcement to ensure that regulations are actually implemented. This is particularly true for the world's high seas, that area outside the 200-mile limit from shore and the jurisdiction of any single country except for loose regulation by the United Nations and international treaties. These waters, covering an area larger than all of the world's continents combined, exemplify the tragedy of the global commons: exploited by all, but protected by none.

Not surprisingly, the absence of effective management regimes to ensure that fish and other ocean resources are not overexploited has taken a huge toll on the world's fisheries. Of the nearly 600 species groups monitored by the United Nations' Food and Agricultural Organization, only 23 percent are not fully overexploited. Many fisheries scientists consider even this estimate to be optimistic. Recent studies suggest that 90 percent of the world's large fish have disappeared, that close to one-third of the world's commercial fisheries have collapsed, and that, unless current trends are reversed, all of the world's remaining commercial fisheries are likely to collapse by 2048.

The picture in the United States is similarly troubling. Only 14 percent of the fisheries under federal management are considered healthy. The other 86 percent are either subject to overfishing at unsustainably high levels or their status is "unknown." Even those fish populations deemed "healthy" are not managed in ways that take into account the needs of their broader ecosystems. Removal of these fish can have potentially negative impacts on other species within those systems.

Compared to damage to terrestrial systems, which is relatively visible and easy to portray to the public, the ongoing destruction of the oceans is far more difficult to communicate. Most of the marine environment is remote, inaccessible and largely beyond the scope of human sensory experience. As a result, the public is far less aware of the crisis affecting the world's oceans than of problems affecting land-based systems. Equally if not more troubling, most people are unaware of the importance of the sea to all life on Earth, the profoundly damaging impacts that human beings are having on the ocean environment, and the potential consequences to both people and nature if these problems continue to be ignored.

The World Is Facing a Global Water Crisis

Maude Barlow

Maude Barlow is an author, the national chairperson of the Council of Canadians, chairperson of Food and Water Watch in the United States, and co-founder of the Blue Planet Project, which advocates for the right to water for all people.

The three water crises—dwindling freshwater supplies, inequitable access to water and the corporate control of water—pose the greatest threat of our time to the planet and to our survival. Together with impending climate change from fossil fuel emissions, the water crises impose some life-or-death decisions on us all. Unless we collectively change our behavior, we are heading toward a world of deepening conflict and potential wars over the dwindling supplies of freshwater—between nations, between rich and poor, between the public and the private interest, between rural and urban populations, and between the competing needs of the natural world and industrialized humans.

Water Is Becoming a Growing Source of Conflict Between Countries

Around the world, more that 215 major rivers and 300 groundwater basins and aquifers are shared by two or more countries, creating tensions over ownership and use of the precious waters they contain. Growing shortages and unequal distribution of water are causing disagreements, sometimes violent, and becoming a security risk in many regions. Britain's former defense secretary, John Reid, warns of coming "water wars." In a public statement on the eve of a 2006 summit on climate change, Reid predicted that violence and political conflict would become more likely as watersheds turn to deserts, glaciers melt and water supplies are poisoned. He went so far as to say that the global water crisis was becoming a global security issue and that Britain's armed forces should be prepared to tackle conflicts, including warfare, over dwindling water sources. "Such changes make the emergence of violent conflict more, rather than less, likely," former British prime minister Tony Blair told *The Independent*. "The blunt truth is that the lack of water and agricultural land is a significant contributory factor to the tragic conflict we see unfolding in Darfur. We should see this as a warning sign."

Water has recently (and suddenly) become a key strategic security and foreign policy priority for the United States.

The Independent gave several other examples of regions of potential conflict. These include Israel, Jordan and Palestine, who all rely on the Jordan River, which is controlled by Israel; Turkey and Syria, where Turkish plans to build dams on the Euphrates River brought the country to the brink of war with Syria in 1998, and where Syria now accuses Turkey of deliberately meddling with its water supply; China and India, where the Brahmaputra River has caused tension between the two countries in the past, and where China's proposal to divert the river is re-igniting the divisions; Angola, Botswana and Namibia, where disputes over the Okavango water basin that have flared in the past are now threatening to re-ignite as Namibia is proposing to build a three hundred-kilometer pipeline that will drain the delta; Ethiopia and Egypt, where population growth is threatening conflict along the Nile; and Bangladesh and India, where flooding in the Ganges caused by melting glaciers in the Himalayas is wreaking havoc in Bangladesh, leading to a rise in illegal, and unpopular, migration to India.

While not likely to lead to armed conflict, stresses are growing along the U.S.-Canadian border over shared boundary waters. In particular, concerns are growing over the future of the Great Lakes, whose waters are becoming increasingly polluted and whose water tables are being steadily drawn down by the huge buildup of population and industry around the basin. A joint commission set up to oversee these waters was recently bypassed by the governors of the American states bordering the Great Lakes, who passed an amendment to the treaty governing the lakes that allows for water diversions to new communities off the basin on the American side. Canadian protests fell on deaf ears in Washington. In 2006, the U.S. government announced plans to have the U.S. coast guard patrol the Great Lakes using machine guns mounted on their vessels and revealed that it had created thirty-four permanent live-fire training zones along the Great Lakes from where it had already conducted a number of automatic weapons drills due to fierce opposition, firing three thousand lead bullets each time into the lakes. The Bush administration has temporarily called off these drills but is already asserting U.S. authority over what has in the past been considered joint waters.

Similar trouble is brewing on the U.S.-Mexican border, where a private group of U.S.-based water rights holders is using the North American Free Trade Agreement to challenge the long-term practice by Mexican farmers to divert water from the Rio Grande before it reaches the United States.

U.S. energy interests in the Middle East could be threatened by water conflicts in the region.

Water Is Becoming a Global Security Issue: The United States

Water has recently (and suddenly) become a key strategic security and foreign policy priority for the United States. In the wake of the terrorist attacks of 9-11, protection of U.S. waterways and drinking water supplies from terrorist attack became vitally important to the White House. When Congress created the Department of Homeland Security in 2002, it gave the department responsibility for securing the nation's water infrastructure and allocated US$548 million in appropriations for security of water infrastructure facilities, funding that was increased in subsequent years. The Environmental Protection Agency created a National Homeland Security Research Center to develop the scientific foundations and tools to be used in the event of an attack on the nation's water systems, and a Water Security Division was established to train water utility personnel on security issues. It also created a Water Information Sharing and Analysis Center for dissemination of alerts about potential threats to drinking water and, with the American Water Works Association, a rapid e-mail notification system for professionals called the Water Security Channel. Ever true to market economy ideology, the Department of Homeland Security's mandate includes promoting public-private partnerships in protecting the nation's water security.

But the interest in water did not stop there. Water is becoming as important a strategic issue as energy in Washington. In an August 2004 briefing note for the Institute for the Analysis of Global Security, a think tank that focuses on the link between energy and security, Dr. Allan R. Hoffman, a senior analyst for the U.S. Department of Energy, declared that the energy security of the United States actually depends on the state of its water resources and warns of a growing water-security crisis worldwide. "Just as energy security became a national priority in the period following the Arab Oil Embargo of 1973–74, water security is destined to become a national and global priority in the decades ahead," says Hoffman. He notes that central to addressing water security issues is finding the energy to extract water from underground aquifers, transport water through pipelines and canals, manage and treat water for reuse and desalinate brackish and sea water—all technologies now being promoted by U.S. government partnerships with American companies. He also points out that the U.S. energy interests in the Middle East could be threatened by water conflicts in the region: "Water conflicts add to the instability of a region on which the U.S. depends heavily for oil.

"Continuation or inflammation of these conflicts could subject U.S. energy supplies to blackmail again, as occurred in the 1970s." Water shortages and global warming pose a "serious threat" to America's national security, top retired military leaders told the president in an April 2007 report published by the national security think tank CNA Corporation. Six retired admirals and five retired generals warned of a future of rampant water wars into which the United States will be dragged. Erik Peterson, director of the Global Strategy Institute of the Center for Strategic and International Studies, a research organization in Washington that calls itself a "strategic planning partner for the government," says that the United States must make water a top priority in foreign policy. "There is a very, very critical dimension to all these global water problems here at home," he told *Voice of America News*. "The first is that it's in our national interest to see stability and security and economic development in key areas of the world, and water is a big factor with that whole set of challenges." His center has joined forces with ITT Industries, the giant water technology company; Proctor & Gamble, which has created a home water purifier called PUR and is working with the UN in a joint public-private venture in developing countries; Coca-Cola; and Sandia National Laboratories to launch a joint-research institute called Global Water Futures (GWF). Sandia, whose motto is "securing a peaceful and free world through technology" and that works to "maintain U.S. military and nuclear superiority," is contracted out to weapons manufacturer Lockheed Martin by the U.S. government, to operate, thus linking water security to military security in a direct way.

The mandate of Global Water Futures is twofold: to affect U.S. strategy and policy regarding the global water crisis and to develop the technology necessary to advance the solution. In a September 2005 report, Global Water Futures warned that the global water crisis is driving the world toward "a tipping point in human history," and elaborated on the need for the United States to start taking water security more seriously: "In light of the global trends in water, it is clear that water quality and water management will affect almost every major U.S. strategic priority in every key region of the world. Addressing the world's water needs will go well beyond humanitarian and economic development interests. . . . Policies focused on water in regions across the planet must be regarded as a critical element in U.S. national security strategy. Such policies should be part of a broader, comprehensive, and integrated U.S. strategy toward the global water challenges."

Humanity still has a chance to head off these scenarios of conflict and war. We could start with a global covenant on water.

Innovations in policy and technology must be tightly linked, says the report, no doubt music to the ears of the corporations that sponsored it. GWF calls for closer innovation and cooperation between governments and the private sector and "redoubled" efforts to mobilize public-private partnerships in the development of technological solutions. And, in language that will be familiar to critics of the Bush administration who argue that the United States is not in Iraq to promote democracy, but rather to secure oil resources and make huge profits for American companies in the "rebuilding" effort, the report links upholding American values of democracy with the profit to be gained in the process: "Water issues are critical to U.S. national security and integral to upholding American values of humanitarianism and democratic development. Moreover, engagement with international water issues guarantees business opportunity for the U.S. private sector, which is well positioned to contribute to development and reap economic reward." Listed among the U.S. government agencies engaged in water issues in the report is the Department of Commerce, which "facilitates U.S. water businesses and market research, and improves U.S. competitiveness in the international water market."

Blue Covenant: The Alternative Water Future

Humanity still has a chance to head off these scenarios of conflict and war. We could start with a global covenant on water. The Blue Covenant should have three components: a water conservation covenant from people and their governments that recognizes the right of the Earth and of other species to clean water, and pledges to protect and conserve the world's water supplies; a water justice covenant between those in the global North who have water and resources and those in the global South who do not, to work in solidarity for water justice, water for all and local control of water; and a water democracy covenant among all governments acknowledging that water is a fundamental human right for all. Therefore, governments are required not only to provide clean water to their citizens as a public service, but they must also recognize that citizens of other countries have the right to water as well and to find peaceful solutions to water disputes between states.

A good example of this is the Good Water Makes Good Neighbors project of Friends of the Earth Middle East, which seeks to use shared water and the notion of water justice to negotiate a wider peace accord in the region. Another example is the successful restoration of the beautiful Lake Constance by Germany, Austria, Lichtenstein and Switzerland, the four countries that share it.

The Blue Covenant should also form the heart of a new covenant on the right to water to be adopted both in nation-state constitutions and in international law at the United Nations. To create the conditions for this covenant will require a concerted and collective international collaboration and will have to tackle all three water crises together with the alternatives: Water Conservation, Water Justice, and Water Democracy.

Overpopulation Is the Central Environmental Crisis Facing the World

Paul R. Ehrlich and Anne H. Ehrlich

Paul R. Ehrlich and Anne H. Ehrlich work in the Department of Biology and the Center for Conservation Biology at Stanford University, where he is a professor of Population Studies and Biological Sciences and she is a senior research associate. Their latest book is The Dominant Animal: Human Evolution and the Environment.

Over some 60 million years, *Homo sapiens* [the scientific name for the human species] has evolved into the dominant animal on the planet, acquiring binocular vision, upright posture, large brains, and—most importantly—language with syntax and that complex store of non-genetic information we call culture. However, in the last several centuries we've increasingly been using our relatively newly acquired power, especially our culturally evolved technologies, to deplete the natural capital of Earth—in particular its deep, rich agricultural soils, its groundwater stored during ice ages, and its biodiversity—as if there were no tomorrow.

Population Growth and Over-Consumption

The point, all too often ignored, is that this trend is being driven in large part by a combination of population growth and increasing per capita consumption, and it cannot be long continued without risking a collapse of our now-global civilization. Too many people—and especially too many politicians and business executives—are under the delusion that such a

Paul R. Ehrlich and Anne H. Ehrlich, "Too Many People, Too Much Consumption," *Yale Environment 360*, August 4, 2008. Copyright © 2008 Yale Environment 360. Reproduced by permission.

disastrous end to the modern human enterprise can be avoided by technological fixes that will allow the population and the economy to grow forever. But if we fail to bring population growth and over-consumption under control—the number of people on Earth is expected to grow from 6.5 billion today to 9 billion by the second half of the 21st century—then we will inhabit a planet where life becomes increasingly untenable because of two looming crises: global heating, and the degradation of the natural systems on which we all depend.

Our species' negative impact on our own life-support systems can be approximated by the equation I=PAT. In that equation, the size of the population (P) is multiplied by the average affluence or consumption per individual (A), and that in turn is multiplied by some measure of the technology (T) that services and drives the consumption. Thus commuting in automobiles powered by subsidized fossil fuels on proliferating freeways creates a much greater T factor than commuting on bikes using simple paths or working at home on a computer network. The product of P, A, and T is Impact (I), a rough estimate of how much humanity is degrading the ecosystem services it depends upon.

There is no technological change we can make that will permit growth in either human numbers or material affluence to continue to expand.

The equation is not rocket science. Two billion people, all else being equal, put more greenhouse gases into the atmosphere than one billion people. Two billion rich people disrupt the climate more than two billion poor people. Three hundred million Americans consume more petroleum than 1.3 billion Chinese. And driving an SUV is using a far more environmentally malign transportation technology than riding mass transit.

Solutions Must Address Global Dangers

The technological dimensions of our predicament—such as the need for alternatives to fossil fuel energy—are frequently discussed if too little acted upon. Judging from media reports and the statements of politicians, environmental problems, to the degree they are recognized, can be solved by minor changes in technologies and recycling (T). Switching to ultra-light, fuel-efficient cars will obviously give some short-term advantage, but as population and consumption grow, they will pour still more carbon dioxide (and vaporized rubber) into the atmosphere and require more natural areas to be buried under concrete. More recycling will help, but many of our society's potentially most dangerous effluents (such as hormone-mimicking chemicals) cannot practically be recycled. There is no technological change we can make that will permit growth in either human numbers or material affluence to continue to expand. In the face of this, the neglect of the intertwined issues of population and consumption is stunning.

Many past human societies have collapsed under the weight of overpopulation and environmental neglect, but today the civilization in peril is global. The population factor in what appears to be a looming catastrophe is even greater than most people suppose. Each person added today to the population on average causes more damage to humanity's critical life-support systems than did the previous addition—everything else being equal. The reason is simple: *Homo sapiens* became the dominant animal by being smart. Farmers didn't settle first on poor soils where water was scarce, but rather in rich river valleys. That's where most cities developed, where rich soils are now being paved over for roads and suburbs, and where water supplies are being polluted or overexploited.

As a result, to support additional people it is necessary to move to ever poorer lands, drill wells deeper, or tap increasingly remote sources to obtain water—and then spend more energy to transport that water ever greater distances to farm fields, homes, and factories. Our distant ancestors could pick up nearly pure copper on Earth's surface when they started to use metals; now people must use vast amounts of energy to mine and smelt gigantic amounts of copper ore of ever poorer quality, some in concentrations of less than one percent. The same can be said for other important metals. And petroleum can no longer be found easily on or near the surface, but must be gleaned from wells drilled a mile or more deep, often in inaccessible localities, such as under continental shelves beneath the sea. All of the paving, drilling, fertilizer manufacturing, pumping, smelting, and transporting needed to provide for the consumption of burgeoning numbers of people produces greenhouse gases and thus tightens the connection between population and climate disruption.

Ignoring Overpopulation and Overconsumption

So why is the topic of overpopulation so generally ignored? There are some obvious reasons. Attempts by governments to limit their nation's population growth are anathema to those on the right who believe the only role for governments in the bedroom is to force women to take unwanted babies to term. Those on the left fear, with some legitimacy, that population control could turn racist or discriminatory in other ways—for example, attempting to reduce the numbers of minorities or the poor. Many fear the specter of more of "them" compared to "us," and all of us fear loss of liberty and economic decline (since population growth is often claimed necessary for economic health). And there are religious leaders who still try to promote over-reproduction by their flocks, though in much of the world their efforts are largely futile (Catholic countries in Europe tend to be low-birthrate leaders, for example).

But much of the responsibility must go to ignorance, which leads mainstream media, even newspapers like *The New York Times*, to maintain a pro-natalist stance. For example, the

Times had an article on June 29 [2008] about a "baby bust" in industrialized countries in which the United States (still growing) was noted as a "sparkling exception." Beyond the media, great foundations have turned their "population programs" away from encouraging low fertility rates and toward topics like "changing sexual mores"—avoiding discussion of the contribution demographics is making to a possible collapse of civilization.

Consumption regulation is a lot more complex than population regulation.

Silence on the overconsumption (Affluence) factor in the I=PAT equation is more readily explained. Consumption is still viewed as an unalloyed good by many economists, along with business leaders and politicians, who tend to see jacking up consumption as a cure-all for economic ills. Too much unemployment? Encourage people to buy an SUV or a new refrigerator. Perpetual growth is the creed of the cancer cell, but third-rate economists can't think of anything else. Some leading economists *are* starting to tackle the issue of overconsumption, but the problem and its cures are tough to analyze. Scientists have yet to develop consumption condoms or morning-after-shopping-spree pills.

And, of course, there are the vexing problems of consumption of people in poor countries. On one hand, a billion or more people have problems of *underconsumption*. Unless their basic needs are met, they are unlikely to be able to make important contributions to attaining sustainability. On the other hand, there is also the issue of the "new consumers" in developing economies such as China and India, where the wealth of a sizable minority is permitting them to acquire the consumption habits (e.g., eating a lot of meat and driving automobiles) of the rich nations. Consumption regulation is a lot more complex than population regulation, and it is much more difficult to find humane and equitable solutions to the problem.

Our Wasted Capacity for the Right Decisions

The dominant animal is wasting its brilliance and its wonderful achievements; civilization's fate is being determined by decision makers who determinedly look the other way in favor of immediate comfort and profit. Thousands of scientists recently participated in a Millennium Ecosystem Assessment that outlined our current environmental dilemma, but the report's dire message made very little impact. Absent attention to that message, the fates of Easter Island, the Classic Maya civilization, and Nineveh—all of which collapsed following environmental degradation—await us all.

We believe it is possible to avoid that global denouement. Such mobilization means developing some consensus on goals—perhaps through a global dialogue in which people discuss the human predicament and decide whether they would like to see a maximum number of people living at a minimum standard of living, or perhaps a much lower population size that gives individuals a broad choice of lifestyles. We have suggested a forum for such a dialogue, modeled partly on the Intergovernmental Panel on Climate Change, but with more "bottom up" participation. It is clear that only widespread changes in norms can give humanity a chance of attaining a sustainable and reasonably conflict-free society.

How to achieve such change—involving everything from demographic policies and transformation of planet-wide energy, industrial, and agricultural systems, to North-South and interfaith relationships and military postures—is a gigantic challenge to everyone. Politicians, industrialists, ecologists, social scientists, everyday citizens, and the media must join this debate. Whether it is possible remains to be seen; societies have managed to make major transitions in the recent past, as the civil rights revolution in the United States and the collapse of communism in the Soviet Union clearly demonstrate.

We'll continue to hope and work for a cultural transformation in how we treat each other and the natural systems we depend upon. We can create a peaceful and sustainable global civilization, but it will require realistic thinking about the problems we face and a new mobilization of political will.

CHAPTER 2

Current
CONTROVERSIES

Is Global Warming a Real Threat?

Chapter Overview

Robert S. Boyd

Robert S. Boyd is a science and technology writer who has worked at the Washington Bureau for over 40 years. He shares a Pulitzer Prize with Clark Hoyt—won for revealing Senator Thomas Eagleton's mental illness background.

Official government measurements show that the world's temperature has cooled a bit since reaching its most recent peak in 1998.

That's given global warming skeptics new ammunition to attack the prevailing theory of climate change. The skeptics argue that the current stretch of slightly cooler temperatures means that costly measures to limit carbon dioxide emissions are ill-founded and unnecessary.

Proposals to combat global warming are "crazy" and will "destroy more than a million good American jobs and increase the average family's annual energy bill by at least $1,500 a year," the Heartland Institute, a conservative research organization based in Chicago, declared in full-page newspaper ads earlier this summer. "High levels of carbon dioxide actually benefit wildlife and human health," the ads asserted.

Warmer Times Ahead

Many scientists agree, however, that hotter times are ahead. A decade of level or slightly lower temperatures is only a temporary dip to be expected as a result of natural, short-term variations in the enormously complex climate system, they say.

"The preponderance of evidence is that global warming will resume," Nicholas Bond, a meteorologist at the National

Robert S. Boyd, "Drop in World Temperatures Fuels Global Warming Debate," *McClatchy Washington Bureau*, August 19, 2009. © McClatchy-Tribune Information Services. All Rights Reserved. Reproduced by permission.

Oceanic and Atmospheric Administration's Pacific Marine Environmental Laboratory in Seattle, said in an e-mail.

"Natural variability can account for the slowing of the global mean temperature rise we have seen," said Jeff Knight, a climate expert at the Hadley Centre for Climate Prediction and Research in Exeter, England.

According to data from the National Space Science and Technology Center in Huntsville, Ala., the global high temperature in 1998 was 0.76 degrees Celsius (1.37 degrees Fahrenheit) above the average for the previous 20 years.

So far this year, the high has been 0.42 degrees Celsius (0.76 degrees Fahrenheit), above the 20-year average, clearly cooler than before.

However, scientists say the skeptics' argument is misleading.

Climate experts say the 1998 record was partly caused by El Niño, a periodic warming of tropical Pacific Ocean waters that affects the climate worldwide.

Cooling Trends Do Not Mean an End to Global Warming

"It's entirely possible to have a period as long as a decade or two of cooling superimposed on the long-term warming trend," said David Easterling, chief of scientific services at NOAA's National Climatic Data Center in Asheville, N.C.

"These short term fluctuations are statistically insignificant (and) entirely due to natural internal variability," Easterling said in an essay published in the journal Geophysical Research Letters in April. "It's easy to 'cherry pick' a period to reinforce a point of view."

Climate experts say the 1998 record was partly caused by El Niño, a periodic warming of tropical Pacific Ocean waters that affects the climate worldwide.

Higher Temperatures in 1998 Were Due to El Niño

"The temperature peak in 1998 to a large extent can be attributed to the very strong El Niño event of 1997-98," Bond said. "Temperatures for the globe as a whole tend to be higher during El Niño, and particularly events as intense as that one."

El Niño is returning this summer after a four-year absence and is expected to hang around until late next year.

"If El Niño continues to strengthen as projected, expect more (high temperature) records to fall," said Thomas Karl, who's the director of the National Climatic Data Center in Asheville.

"At least half of the years after 2009 will be warmer than 1998, the warmest year currently on record," predicted Jeff Knight, a climate variability expert at the Hadley Centre in England.

John Christy, the director of the Earth System Science Center at the University of Alabama in Huntsville, who often sides with the skeptics, agreed that the recent cooling won't last.

"The atmosphere is just now feeling the bump in tropical Pacific temperatures related to El Niño," Christy said in an e-mail. As a result, July experienced "the largest one-month jump in our 31-year record of global satellite temperatures. We should see a warmer 2009-2010 due to El Niño."

The Need to Know More

Christy added, however: "Our ignorance of the climate system is still enormous, and our policy makers need to know that . . . We really don't know much about what causes multi-year changes like this."

In addition to newspaper ads, the Heartland Institute sponsors conferences, books, papers, videos and Web sites arguing its case against the global warming threat.

The skeptics include scientists such as Richard Lindzen, a meteorologist at the Massachusetts Institute of Technology, who thinks that climate science is too uncertain to justify drastic measures to control CO_2. He calls the case for action against global warming "silly" and "grotesque."

In reality, global warming "never ceased," said Karl, the climate data center director.

Others go further. For example, Don Easterbrook, a geologist at Western Washington University in Bellingham, thinks the world is in a 30-year cooling phase.

"The most recent global warming that began in 1977 is over, and the Earth has entered a new phase of global cooling," Easterbrook said in a talk to the American Geophysical Union's annual meeting in San Francisco in December.

Government scientists strongly disagree. "Claims that global warming is not occurring . . . ignore this natural variability and are misleading," said NOAA's Easterling.

In reality, global warming "never ceased," said Karl, the climate data center director.

Global Warming Is the Greatest Threat Humans Have Ever Faced

Bill McKibben

Bill McKibben is an American environmentalist and writer who frequently writes about global warming, alternative energy, and the need for more localized economies.

Here's how it works. Before the industrial revolution, the Earth's atmosphere contained about 280 parts per million of carbon dioxide [CO_2]. That was a good amount—"good" defined as "what we were used to." Since the molecular structure of carbon dioxide traps heat near the planet's surface that would otherwise radiate back out to space, civilization grew up in a world whose thermostat was set by that number. It equated to a global average temperature of about 57 degrees Fahrenheit (about 14 degrees Celsius), which in turn equated to all the places we built our cities, all the crops we learned to grow and eat, all the water supplies we learned to depend on, even the passage of the seasons that, at higher latitudes, set our psychological calendars.

Once we started burning coal and gas and oil to power our lives, that 280 number started to rise. When we began measuring in the late 1950s, it had already reached the 315 level. Now it's at 380, and increasing by roughly two parts per million annually. That doesn't sound like very much, but it turns out that the extra heat that CO_2 traps, a couple of watts per square meter of the Earth's surface, is enough to warm the planet considerably. We've raised the temperature more than a degree Fahrenheit (0.56 degrees Celsius) already. It's impossible to precisely predict the consequences of any further increase in CO_2 in the atmosphere. But the warming we've seen so far has started almost everything frozen on Earth to melting; it has changed seasons and rainfall patterns; it's set the sea to rising.

A Lot of Carbon

No matter what we do now, that warming will increase some—there's a lag time before the heat fully plays out in the atmosphere. That is, we can't stop global warming. Our task is less inspiring: to contain the damage, to keep things from getting out of control. And even that is not easy. For one thing, until recently there's been no clear data suggesting the point where catastrophe looms. Now we're getting a better picture—the past couple of years have seen a series of reports indicating that 450 parts per million CO_2 is a threshold we'd be wise to respect. Beyond that point, scientists believe future centuries will likely face the melting of the Greenland and West Antarctic ice sheets and a subsequent rise in sea level of giant proportion. Four hundred fifty parts per million is still a best guess (and it doesn't include the witches' brew of other, lesser, greenhouse gases like methane and nitrous oxide). But it will serve as a target of sorts for the world to aim at. A target that's moving, fast. If concentrations keep increasing by two parts per million per year, we're only three and a half decades away. So the math isn't complicated—but that doesn't mean it isn't intimidating. So far only the Europeans and Japanese have even begun to trim their carbon emissions, and they may not meet their own modest targets. Meanwhile, U.S. carbon emissions, a quarter of the world's total, continue to rise steadily—earlier this year [2007] we told the United Nations [UN] we'd be producing 20 percent more carbon in 2020 than we had in 2000. China and India are suddenly starting to produce huge quantities of CO_2 as well. On a per capita basis (which is really the only sensible way to think about the morality of the situation), they aren't anywhere close to American figures, but their populations are so huge, and their economic growth so rapid, that they make the prospect of a worldwide decline in emissions seem much more daunting. The Chinese are currently building a coal-fired power plant every week or so. That's a lot of carbon.

Everyone involved knows what the basic outlines of a deal that could avert catastrophe would look like: rapid, sustained, and dramatic cuts in emissions by the technologically advanced countries, coupled with large-scale technology transfer to China, India, and the rest of the developing world so that they can power up their emerging economies without burning up their coal. Everyone knows the big questions, too: Are such rapid cuts even possible? Do we have the political will to make them and to extend them overseas?

Many of the paths to stabilization run straight through our daily lives, and in every case they will demand difficult changes.

Are Rapid Cuts in Emissions Possible?

The first question—is it even possible—is usually addressed by fixating on some single new technology (hydrogen! ethanol!) and imagining it will solve our troubles. But the scale of the problem means we'll need many strategies. Three years ago a Princeton team made one of the best assessments of the possibilities. Stephen Pacala and Robert Socolow published a paper in *Science* detailing 15 stabilization wedges—changes big enough to really matter, and for which the technology was already available or clearly on the horizon. Most people have heard of some of them: more fuel-efficient cars, better-built homes, wind turbines, biofuels like ethanol. Others are newer and, less sure: plans for building coal-fired power plants that can separate carbon from the exhaust so it can be "sequestered" underground.

These approaches have one thing in common: They're more difficult than simply burning fossil fuel. They force us to realize that we've already had our magic fuel and that what comes next will be more expensive and more difficult. The price tag for the global transition will be in the trillions of dollars. Of course, along the way it will create myriad new jobs, and when it's complete, it may be a much more elegant system. (Once you've built the windmill, the wind is free; you don't need to guard it against terrorists or build a massive army to control the countries from which it blows.) And since we're wasting so much energy now, some of the first tasks would be relatively easy. If we replaced every incandescent bulb that burned out in the next decade anyplace in the world with a compact fluorescent, we'd make an impressive start on one of the 15 wedges. But in that same decade we'd need to build 400,000 large wind turbines—clearly possible, but only with real commitment. We'd need to follow the lead of Germany and Japan and seriously subsidize rooftop solar panels; we'd need to get most of the world's farmers plowing their fields less, to build back the carbon their soils have lost. We'd need to do everything all at once. As precedents for such collective effort, people sometimes point to the Manhattan Project to build a nuclear weapon or the Apollo Program to put a man on the moon. But those analogies don't really work. They demanded the intense concentration of money and intelligence on a single small niche in our technosphere. Now we need almost the opposite: a commitment to take what we already know how to do and somehow spread it into every corner of our economies, and indeed our most basic activities. It's as if NASA's goal had been to put all of us on the moon.

Not all the answers are technological, of course—maybe not even most of them. Many of the paths to stabilization run straight through our daily lives, and in every case they will demand difficult changes. Air travel is one of the fastest growing sources of carbon emissions around the world, for instance, but even many of us who are noble about changing lightbulbs and happy to drive hybrid cars chafe at the thought of not jetting around the country or the world. By now we're used to ordering take-out food from every corner of the world every night of our lives—according to one study, the average bite of food has traveled nearly 1,500 miles (2,414 kilometers) before it reaches an American's lips, which means it's been marinated in (crude) oil. We drive alone, because it's more convenient than adjusting our schedules for public transit. We build ever bigger homes even as our family sizes shrink, and we watch ever bigger TVs, and—well, enough said. We need to figure out how to change those habits.

We Must Make Sacrifices

Probably the only way that will happen is if fossil fuel costs us considerably more. All the schemes to cut carbon emissions— the so-called cap-and-trade systems, for instance, that would let businesses bid for permission to emit—are ways to make coal and gas and oil progressively more expensive, and thus to change the direction in which economic gravity pulls when it applies to energy. If what we paid for a gallon of gas reflected even a portion of its huge environmental cost, we'd be driving small cars to the train station, just like the Europeans. And we'd be riding bikes when the sun shone.

In the end, global warming presents the greatest test we humans have yet faced.

The most straightforward way to raise the price would be a tax on carbon. But that's not easy. Since everyone needs to use fuel, it would be regressive—you'd have to figure out how to keep from hurting poor people unduly. And we'd need to be grown-up enough to have a real conversation about taxes— say, about switching away from taxes on things we like (employment) to taxes on things we hate (global warming). That may be too much to ask for—but if it is, then what chance is there we'll be able to take on the even more difficult task of persuading the Chinese, the Indians, and all who are lined up behind them to forgo a coal-powered future in favor of something more manageable? We know it's possible—earlier this year a UN panel estimated that the total cost for the energy transition, once all the pluses and minuses were netted out, would be just over 0.1 percent of the world's economy each year for the next quarter century. A small price to pay.

In the end, global warming presents the greatest test we humans have yet faced. Are we ready to change, in dramatic and prolonged ways, in order to offer a workable future to subsequent generations and diverse forms of life? If we are, new technologies and new habits offer some promise. But only if we move quickly and decisively—and with a maturity we've rarely shown as a society or a species. It's our coming-of-age moment, and there are no certainties or guarantees. Only a window of possibility, closing fast but still ajar enough to let in some hope.

Global Warming Could Lead to World Poverty and War

Brad Knickerbocker

Brad Knickerbocker is a staff writer for The Christian Science Monitor.

For years, the debate over global warming has focused on the three big "E's": environment, energy, and economic impact. [In April 2007] it officially entered the realm of national security threats and avoiding wars as well.

A platoon of retired US generals and admirals warned that global warming "presents significant national security challenges to the United States." The United Nations Security Council held its first ever debate on the impact of climate change on conflicts. And in Congress, a bipartisan bill would require a National Intelligence Estimate by all federal intelligence agencies to assess the security threats posed by global climate change.

Many experts view climate change as a "threat multiplier" that intensifies instability around the world by worsening water shortages, food insecurity, disease, and flooding that lead to forced migration. That's the thrust of a 35-page report by 11 admirals and generals issued by the Alexandria, Va.-based national security think tank The CNA Corporation. The study, titled National Security and the Threat of Climate Change, predicts:

"Projected climate change will seriously exacerbate already marginal living standards in many Asian, African, and Middle Eastern nations, causing widespread political instability and the likelihood of failed states. . . . The chaos that results can be an incubator of civil strife, genocide, and the growth of terrorism.

"The U.S. may be drawn more frequently into these situations, either alone or with allies, to help provide stability before conditions worsen and are exploited by extremists. The U.S. may also be called upon to undertake stability and reconstruction efforts once a conflict has begun, to avert further disaster and reconstitute a stable environment."

We will pay to reduce greenhouse gas emissions today . . . or we'll pay the price later in military terms.

Paying the Price Now or Later

"We will pay for this one way or another," retired Marine Gen. Anthony Zinni, former commander of American forces in the Middle East and one of the report's authors, told the *Los Angeles Times*. "We will pay to reduce greenhouse gas emissions today . . . or we'll pay the price later in military terms. And that will involve human lives."

As quoted in the *Associated Press*, British Foreign Secretary Margaret Beckett, who presided over the UN meeting in New York April 17 [2007], posed the question "What makes wars start?" The answer:

"Fights over water. Changing patterns of rainfall. Fights over food production, land use. There are few greater potential threats to our economies . . . but also to peace and security itself."

This is the concern behind a recently introduced bipartisan bill by Sens. Richard Durbin (D) of Illinois and Chuck Hagel (R) of Nebraska. It would require all US intelligence agencies—the CIA, the NSA, the Pentagon, and the FBI—to conduct a comprehensive review of potential security threats related to climate change around the world.

"Many of the most severe effects of global warming are expected in regions where fragile governments are least capable of responding to them," Senator Durbin said in a story from the *Inter Press Service* news agency in Rome. "Failing to recognize and plan for the geopolitical consequences of global warming would be a serious mistake."

Rep. Edward J. Markey (D) of Massachusetts, chairman of the newly formed House Select Committee on Energy Independence and Global Warming, is proposing companion legislation that would fund climate change plans by the Department of Defense. On his website, Mr. Markey called for action based on the retired senior officers' report, saying:

"Global warming's impacts on natural resources and climate systems may create the fiercest battle our world has ever seen. If we don't cut pollution and head off severe global warming at the pass, we could see extreme geopolitical strain over decreased clean water, environmental refugees, and other impacts."

In a speech April 16 [2007] to BritishAmerican Business Inc., a trans-Atlantic business organization, British Foreign Secretary Beckett "praised the growing actions of US business executives and state politicians in addressing climate change, including California Governor Arnold Schwarzenegger, who along with British Prime Minister Tony Blair announced plans last year to work toward a possible joint emissions-trading market," reported the *Associated Press*.

Ms. Beckett also told the business executives that clean technology is going to create "massive" market opportunities:

"Those who move into that market first—first to design, first to patent, first to sell, first to invest, first to build a brand—have an unparalleled chance to make money."

The Bush administration has taken a less stark view of the security implications of greenhouse-gas emissions than many scientists and military officers.

These challenges are not traditional national security concerns, such as the conflict of arms or ideologies.

But in a broader context, the administration has agreed that environmental issues could present national and international security challenges. In its 2006 National Security Strategy, the administration acknowledged that environmental destruction, including that caused by human activity, "may overwhelm the capacity of local authorities to respond, and may even overtax national militaries, requiring a larger international response."

"These challenges are not traditional national security concerns, such as the conflict of arms or ideologies. But if left unaddressed they can threaten national security."

These concerns are likely to keep growing and continue to be on the agendas at international meetings.

A strongly worded draft communiqué or June's [2007] G8 summit in Heiligendamm, Germany, warns that "tackling climate change is an imperative, not a choice," reported the British newspaper *The Independent on Sunday*. The draft says:

"Global warming caused largely by human activities is accelerating [and it] will seriously damage our common natural environment and severely weaken [the] global economy, with implications for international security."

It May Already Be
Too Late to Save the Planet
from Global Warming

Michael McCarthy

Michael McCarthy is the environment editor for The Independent, *a British newspaper.*

The world has already passed the point of no return for climate change, and civilisation as we know it is now unlikely to survive, according to James Lovelock, the scientist
and green guru who conceived the idea of Gaia—the Earth
which keeps itself fit for life.

In a profoundly pessimistic new assessment, published in
[the January 16, 2006 issue of] *The Independent*, Professor
Lovelock suggests that efforts to counter global warming cannot succeed, and that, in effect, it is already too late.

The world and human society face disaster to a worse extent, and on a faster timescale, than almost anybody realises,
he believes. He writes: "Before this century is over, billions of
us will die, and the few breeding pairs of people that survive
will be in the Arctic where the climate remains tolerable."

The Revenge of Gaia

In making such a statement, far gloomier than any yet made
by a scientist of comparable international standing, Professor
Lovelock accepts he is going out on a limb. But as the man
who conceived the first wholly new way of looking at life on
Earth since Charles Darwin, he feels his own analysis of what
is happening leaves him no choice. He believes that it is the
self-regulating mechanism of Gaia itself—increasingly ac-
cepted by other scientists worldwide, although they prefer to

Michael McCarthy, "Environment in Crisis: 'We Are Past the Point of No Return,'" *The Independent*, January 16, 2006. Reproduced by permission.

term it the Earth System—which, perversely, will ensure that the warming cannot be mastered.

The harmful consequences of human beings damaging the living planet's ancient regulatory system will be non-linear—in other words, likely to accelerate uncontrollably.

This is because the system contains myriad feedback mechanisms which in the past have acted in concert to keep the Earth much cooler than it otherwise would be. Now, however, they will come together to amplify the warming being caused by human activities such as transport and industry through huge emissions of greenhouse gases such as carbon dioxide (CO_2).

It means that the harmful consequences of human beings damaging the living planet's ancient regulatory system will be non-linear—in other words, likely to accelerate uncontrollably.

He terms this phenomenon "The Revenge of Gaia" and examines it in detail in a . . . book with that [same] title. . . .

The uniqueness of the Lovelock viewpoint is that it is holistic, rather than reductionist. Although he is a committed supporter of current research into climate change, especially at Britain's Hadley Centre, he is not looking at individual facets of how the climate behaves, as other scientists inevitably are. Rather, he is looking at how the whole control system of the Earth behaves when put under stress.

Professor Lovelock, who conceived the idea of Gaia in the 1970s while examining the possibility of life on Mars for NASA in the US, has been warning of the dangers of climate change since major concerns about it first began nearly 20 years ago.

He was one of a select group of scientists who gave an initial briefing on global warming to Margaret Thatcher's Cabinet at 10 Downing Street in April 1989.

Preparing for a Hell of a Climate

His concerns have increased steadily since then, as evidence of a warming climate has mounted. For example, he shared the alarm of many scientists at the news last September [2005] that the ice covering the Arctic Ocean is now melting so fast that in 2005 it reached a historic low point.

[Scientist James Lovelock] is calling on governments . . . to begin large-scale preparations for surviving . . . "a hell of a climate."

[In 2004] . . . he sparked a major controversy with an article in *The Independent* calling on environmentalists to drop their long-standing opposition to nuclear power, which does not produce the greenhouses gases of conventional power stations.

Global warming was proceeding so fast that only a major expansion of nuclear power could bring it under control, he said. Most of the Green movement roundly rejected his call, and does so still.

Now his concerns have reached a peak—and have a new emphasis. Rather than calling for further ways of countering climate change, he is calling on governments in Britain and elsewhere to begin large-scale preparations for surviving what he now sees as inevitable—in his own phrase today, "a hell of a climate", likely to be in Europe up to 8C [degrees Celsius] hotter than it is today.

In his book's concluding chapter, he writes: "What should a sensible European government be doing now? I think we have little option but to prepare for the worst, and assume that we have passed the threshold."

And in [a 2006 article in the] . . . *Independent* he writes: "We will do our best to survive, but sadly I cannot see the United States or the emerging economies of China and India cutting back in time, and they are the main source of [CO_2] emissions. The worst will happen . . ."

"Global dimming" . . . is thought to be holding the global temperature down by several degrees.

He goes on: "We have to keep in mind the awesome pace of change and realise how little time is left to act, and then each community and nation must find the best use of the resources they have to sustain civilisation for as long as they can." He believes that the world's governments should plan to secure energy and food supplies in the global hothouse, and defences against the expected rise in sea levels. The scientist's vision of what human society may ultimately be reduced to through climate change is "a broken rabble led by brutal warlords."

Professor Lovelock draws attention to one aspect of the warming threat in particular, which is that the expected temperature rise is currently being held back artificially by a global aerosol—a layer of dust in the atmosphere right around the planet's northern hemisphere—which is the product of the world's industry.

This shields us from some of the sun's radiation in a phenomenon which is known as "global dimming" and is thought to be holding the global temperature down by several degrees. But with a severe industrial downturn, the aerosol could fall out of the atmosphere in a very short time, and the global temperature could take a sudden enormous leap upwards.

One of the most striking ideas in his book is that of "a guidebook for global warming survivors" aimed at the humans who would still be struggling to exist after a total societal collapse.

Written, not in electronic form, but "on durable paper with long-lasting print", it would contain the basic accumulated scientific knowledge of humanity, much of it utterly taken for granted by us now, but originally won only after a hard struggle—such as our place in the solar system, or the fact that bacteria and viruses cause infectious diseases.

Global warming . . . is almost certainly the greatest threat that mankind has ever faced, because it puts a question mark over the very habitability of the Earth.

The Rough Guide to a Planet in Jeopardy

Global warming, caused principally by the large-scale emissions of industrial gases such as carbon dioxide (CO_2), is almost certainly the greatest threat that mankind has ever faced, because it puts a question mark over the very habitability of the Earth.

Over the coming decades soaring temperatures will mean agriculture may become unviable over huge areas of the world where people are already poor and hungry; water supplies for millions or even billions may fail. Rising sea levels will destroy substantial coastal areas in low-lying countries such as Bangladesh, at the very moment when their populations are mushrooming. Numberless environmental refugees will overwhelm the capacity of any agency, or indeed any country, to cope, while modern urban infrastructure will face devastation from powerful extreme weather events, such as Hurricane Katrina which hit New Orleans last summer [2005].

The international community accepts the reality of global warming, supported by the UN's [United Nations'] Intergovernmental Panel on Climate Change [IPCC]. In its last report, in 2001, the IPCC said global average temperatures were likely to rise by up to 5.8C by 2100. In high latitudes, such as Britain, the rise is likely to be much higher, perhaps 8C. The warming seems to be proceeding faster than anticipated and in the IPCC's next report, 2007, the timescale may be shortened. Yet there still remains an assumption that climate change is controllable, if CO_2 emissions can be curbed. Lovelock is warning: think again.

Global Warming Is Not a Crisis

Philip Stott

Philip Stott is an emeritus professor from the University of London, in the United Kingdom. For the past eighteen years he was editor of the Journal of Biogeography.

From the Babylon of Gilgamesh to the post-Eden of Noah, every age has viewed climate change cataclysmically, as retribution for human greed and sinfulness.

In the 1970s, the fear was "global cooling." The *Christian Science Monitor* then declaimed, "Warning: Earth's climate is changing faster than even experts expect," while *The New York Times* announced, "A major cooling of the climate is widely considered inevitable." Sound familiar? Global warming represents the latest doom-laden "crisis," one demanding sacrifice to Gaia for our wicked fossil-fuel-driven ways.

But neither history nor science bolsters such an apocalyptic faith.

Past and Present Evidence Does Not Point to a Crisis

Extreme weather events are ever present, and there is no evidence of systematic increases. Outside the tropics, variability should decrease in a warmer world. If this is a "crisis," then the world is in permanent "crisis," but will be less prone to "crisis" with warming.

Sea levels have been rising since the end of the last ice age, most rapidly about 12,000 years ago. In recent centuries, the average rate has been relatively uniform. The rate was higher during the first half of the 20th century than during the second. At around a couple of millimeters per year, it is a residual of much larger positive and negative changes locally. The risk from global warming is less than that from other factors (primarily geological).

The impact on agriculture is equivocal. India warmed during the second half of the 20th century, yet agricultural output increased markedly. The impact on disease is dubious. Infectious diseases, like malaria, are not so much a matter of temperature as of poverty and public health. Malaria remains endemic in Siberia, and was once so in Michigan and Europe. Exposure to cold is generally more dangerous.

So, does the claim that humans are the primary cause of recent warming imply "crisis"? The impact on temperature per unit CO_2 [carbon dioxide] goes down, not up, with increasing CO_2. The role of human-induced greenhouse gases does not relate directly to emission rate, nor even to CO_2 levels, but rather to the radiative (or greenhouse) impact. Doubling CO_2 is a convenient benchmark. It is claimed, on the basis of computer models, that this should lead to 1.1–6.4 C [degress Celsius] warming.

What is rarely noted is that we are already three-quarters of the way into this in terms of radiative forcing, but we have only witnessed a 0.6 (+/−0.2) C rise, and there is no reason to suppose that all of this is due to humans.

There is no way we can predictably manage this most complex of coupled, nonlinear chaotic [climate] systems.

Indeed the system requires no external driver to fluctuate by a fraction of a degree because of ocean disequilibrium with the atmosphere. There are also alternative drivers relating to cosmic rays, the sun, water vapor and clouds. Moreover, it is worth remembering that modelers even find it difficult to account for the medieval warm period.

The Real Crisis

Our so-called "crisis" is thus neither a product of current observations nor of projections.

The inconvenient truth is that "doing something" [about climate change] ... and "not doing something" ... are equally unpredictable.

But does it matter if global warming is a "crisis" or not? Aren't we threatened by a serious temperature rise? Shouldn't we act anyway, because we are stewards of the environment?

Herein lies the moral danger behind global warming hysteria. Each day, 20,000 people in the world die of waterborne diseases. Half a billion people go hungry. A child is orphaned by AIDS every seven seconds. This does not have to happen. We allow it while fretting about "saving the planet." What is wrong with us that we downplay this human misery before our eyes and focus on events that will probably not happen even a hundred years hence? We know that the greatest cause of environmental degradation is poverty; on this, we can and must act.

The global warming "crisis" is misguided. In hubristically seeking to "control" climate, we foolishly abandon age-old adaptations to inexorable change. There is no way we can predictably manage this most complex of coupled, nonlinear chaotic systems. The inconvenient truth is that "doing something" (emitting gases) at the margins and "not doing something" (not emitting gases) are equally unpredictable.

Climate change is a norm, not an exception. It is both an opportunity and a challenge. The real crises for 4 billion people in the world remain poverty, dirty water and the lack of a modern energy supply. By contrast, global warming represents an ecochondria of the pampered rich.

We can no longer afford to cling to the anti-human doctrines of outdated environmentalist thinking. The "crisis" is the global warming political agenda, not climate change.

There Is No Scientific Consensus on Global Warming

Wes Vernon

Wes Vernon is a Washington-based writer and veteran broadcast journalist.

"**M**an-made Global Warming," thy name is fraud.

Yet, fraud is precisely what the nation's indoctrination centers—excuse me, schools—are drumming into the heads of young Americans.

Mark Colley, who lives just south of Salt Lake City, learned a few months ago that his middle school daughter had been shown [former vice president and environmental activist] Al Gore's film *An Inconvenient Truth* in her middle school class—without any rebuttal.

When he protested, he was told it was hard to find scientific opinion that does not accept the tenet of man-made "climate change." (Note: With much of the nation buried in snow this winter [2008], the alarmists have quietly replaced the term "global warming" with the new mantra of "climate change," a tactic worthy of Stalinism in World War II—i.e., Hitler bad—now Hitler good—i.e., ooops! Hitler bad again.)

Perhaps the school officials had heard Gore or one of his acolytes intone that "the debate is over" on Global Warming.

Oh, but it is not over, you see.

Comes now this headline in the Canadian *National Post*: "Forget global warming—Welcome to the new Ice Age."

Therein, we learn that snow-cover over North America and much of Siberia, Mongolia, and China is greater than at

Wes Vernon, "The New 'Inconvenient Truth' That Dares Not Say Its Name," *Renew America*, March 17, 2008. Reproduced by permission.

any time since 1966. There have even been most unusual snowfalls in Saudi Arabia—obviously, a shock to the desert natives and their camels.

Tired of Alarmist Propaganda

While Al Gore was making a nice living flying about in jets, essentially lecturing the rest of us about what wasteful slobs we had become, there was information that in his baronial mansion, the electricity use alone was outpacing that of the great unwashed times twenty.

Hypocrisy per se is not the issue here. It is pretty well established that Al Gore is to energy conservation what Eliot Spitzer [the former governor of New York who resigned due to scandal in 2008] is to "Mr. Clean."

Rather, the issue is fact—pure fact. And in honor of that pesky (dare we say "inconvenient?") quality, some 500 unbrainwashed attendees gathered in New York City early this month [March 2008] to put to rest the Gore-style alarmism.

Among the unconvinced was a team of international scientists who formed a new group—the "Nongovernmental International Panel of Climate Change [NIPCC]" It will counter the propaganda disseminated by the United Nations [UN]. By the way, some scientists from the UN showed up at the conference to register their dissent from the alarmists' article of faith on global warming, aka "climate change."

Hundreds of climate experts from around the world . . . issued a "Manhattan Declaration," whose title [is] . . . Nature, not Human Activity, Rules the Climate.

The Scientists Speak

The headline immediately above conveys a message of "Listen up, this is the Holy Writ handing down the tablets from on high." Therefore, it naturally follows that such impudence actually appeared over an editorial in the *New York Times*, entreating its readers to pay heed to UN "scientists" parroting the global warming line of "Help! We're all going to die." Such worthies no doubt covet a Nobel prize like the one awarded Al Gore by the puffed up establishmentarians who peer down their snoots at anyone daring to question their sacrosanct outdated wisdoms.

So we here will crib the *New York Times* headline, and intone (can't quite mimic the super baritone tablet-like echo chamber worthy of the *NYT*—complete with the requisite thunder and lightning—but here goes). "The Scientists Speak!"

Hundreds of climate experts from around the world at the New York conference issued a "Manhattan, Declaration," whose title gets right to the bottom line: *Nature, not Human Activity, Rules the Climate.*

Among those at the gathering was former UN scientist (he quit the UN group in disgust) Dr. Paul Reiter of the Pasteur Institute in Paris. Dr. Reiter told the attendees that, "[a]s far as the science being 'settled,' I think that is an obscenity. The fact is the science is being distorted by those who are not scientists."

Added famed hurricane expert and meteorologist Dr. William Gray: "There are a lot of skeptics out there, all over the U.S. and the rest of the world. [Global warming] has been over-hyped tremendously; most of the climate change we have seen is largely natural. I think we are brainwashing our children terribly."

Those are just two examples of what was authoritatively said at the gathering near Times Square.

Among the findings of the Manhattan Declaration are that (1) there is no convincing evidence that CO_2 [carbon dioxide] emissions from modern industrial activity have caused in the past, or will cause in the future, catastrophic climate change; (2) attempts by governments to inflict taxes and costly regulations on industry and individual citizens with the aim of reducing emissions of CO_2 will pointlessly curtail the prosperity of the West and the progress of developing nations without affecting the climate, and (3) human-caused climate change is not a global crisis.

Obstacles to the Right Discussion

Getting the facts out via the Manhattan Declaration, however, will take some doing. It can be picked up by talk radio, *Fox News*, and conservative websites such as this one.

The Herculean part of the undertaking will be aiming for meaningful coverage in the mainstream media, many of whose lions at the gate were schooled in the Ivy League halls of the Hate America culture.

Not satisfied with stubbornly dragging their feet on granting oil drilling rights in Alaska's ANWR [Arctic National Wildlife Refuge], the worthies of [Speaker of the House] Nancy Pelosi's Capitol Hill fiefdom are now out to *stop* the sale of any drilling rights in the Chukchi Sea—just south of the Arctic Ocean and west of Alaska. The polar bears, you know.

Temperatures over the last decade have not followed [the United Nations Intergovernmental Panel on Climate Change's] models.

The National Oceanic and Atmospheric Administration (NOAA) says Alaskan temperatures are not climbing. The *DeWeese Report* quotes Dr. Mitchell Taylor—a biologist (and another scientist who "speaks") as saying "polar bears are not going extinct," nor do they appear to be "affected" by any "climate change."

Nonetheless, there has been constant pressure from UN climate organizations and wing-nut groups such as Greenpeace to con the EPA [U.S. Environmental Protection Agency]—already a hotbed of career alarmists—into adding the polar bear to its "endangered species" list.

David Wojick, an expert reviewer for the UN Intergovernmental Panel on Climate Change (and thus, a veteran of the "belly of the beast"), said the following:

"The hypothesis that solar variability and not human activity is warming oceans goes a long way to explain the puzzling idea that the Earth's surface may be warming while the atmosphere is not. The [greenhouse gas] hypothesis does not do this. The public is not well served by this constant drumbeat of false alarms fed by computer models manipulated by advocates."

Senator Inhofe Fights the Good Fight

Senator James Inhofe is playing a key role in exposing the man-made "global warming" hoax. He has been out front both as ranking member and former chairman of the Senate Committee on Environment and Public Works.

[The] effort at the use of a fraud scare to sock you with higher taxes is known as "cap-and-trade" legislation.

Praising the participants in the Manhattan Declaration, the Oklahoma Republican noted that the thinking reflected at the New York conference was in sync with much of what was detailed in the senator's own report released in December. The two documents, Inhofe noted, debunk "the endless claims that there is a 'consensus' regarding man-made global warming. In addition, the fact that temperatures over the last decade have not followed [the United Nations Intergovernmental Panel on Climate Change's] models is yet another inconvenient development for the promoters of climate fear. Simply put, the claims by former Vice President Al Gore and the establishment media grow less and less credible every day."

Then Senator Inhofe referenced a scheme to leverage the "global warming" fear to impose "the largest tax increase ever in U.S. history without any measurable climate benefits."

That effort at the use of a fraud scare to sock you with higher taxes is known as "cap-and-trade" legislation. We're out of space for now, but this column needs to explore that particular parcel of enormous mischief to your wallet or purse . . . Later.

The United Nations' Climate Reports Are Full of Errors

Christopher Monckton

Christopher Monckton is an international business consultant specializing in the investigation of scientific frauds.

I earned my Nobel Peace Prize by making the United Nations [UN] fix a deliberate error in its latest climate assessment. After the scientists had finalized the draft, UN bureaucrats inserted a new table, but with four decimal points right-shifted. The bureaucrats had multiplied tenfold the true contribution of the Greenland and West Antarctic ice sheets to sea-level rise. Were they trying to support Al Gore's fantasy that these two ice-sheets would imminently cause sea level to rise 20ft, displacing tens of millions worldwide?

How do we know the UN's error was deliberate? The table, as it first appeared, said the units for sea-level rise were being changed. But the table was new. There was nothing to change from. I wrote to the UN that this misconduct was unacceptable. Two days later, the bureaucracy corrected, relabeled and moved the table, and quietly posted the new version on its Web site. The two ice sheets will contribute, between them, over 100 years, just two and a half inches to sea-level rise. Gore had exaggerated a hundredfold; the UN tenfold. Hawaii is not about to disappear beneath the waves.

The High Court in London recently ordered the British Government to correct nine of the 36 serious errors in Al Gore's climate movie before innocent pupils were exposed to it. It was Gore who, in 1994, announced that Mars was covered in canals full of water. This notion had been disproved before his birth. It was Gore who recently spent $4 million of the profits from his sci-fi comedy horror movie on a luxury condo just feet from the supposedly rising ocean at Fisherman's Wharf, San Francisco. No surprise that he and the mad scientists with whom he has close financial and political links are under investigation for racketeering—peddling a false prospectus to investors in his "green" investment corporation by distorting climate science even after the UK judge's ruling.

Inaccurate Climate Models

It is not so well known that the UN's climate reports are also error-packed and misleading.

To begin with, the UN denies that global temperatures were warmer than today in the medieval warm period. It overlooks the dozens of peer-reviewed papers that establish this fact, and continues to rely on the bogus and now-discredited "hockey-stick" graph by which its previous assessment in 2001 had tried to rewrite history.

> *The scientific debate centers not ... on whether adding CO_2 [carbon dioxide] to the atmosphere will cause warmer weather (it will), but instead on how much warmer the weather will be.*

It was also warmer than today in Roman times, and in the Minoan warm period or Holocene climate optimum, when temperatures were warmer than today for 2000 years in the Bronze Age, firing the emergence of great civilizations worldwide. In each of the four previous interglacial periods, temperatures were 10F [degrees Fahrenheit] warmer than today's. For most of the past half billion years, temperatures were nearly always 12.5F warmer than the present. So the warming that has now stopped (there has been no statistically significant warming since 1998) was well within the natural variability of the climate.

The only chapters in the UN's 1,600-page ramblings that are worth close analysis are those which consider "climate sensitivity"—how big is the effect of greenhouse gases on temperature? The scientific debate centers not, as the Greens try to suggest, on whether adding CO_2 to the atmosphere will cause warmer weather (it will), but instead on how much warmer the weather will be. So the only variable that truly matters in this debate is lambda—the "climate sensitivity parameter." Here are just some of the UN's errors and exaggerations in calculating lambda.

First and foremost, the UN's crafty definition of lambda allows it to overlook the fact that the oceans—1,100 times denser than the atmosphere at the surface, and many times denser still at depth—soak up a good proportion of any additional radiant energy in the atmosphere. The oceans cancel a great deal of "global warming," because the next Ice Age will arrive long before the oceans lose their capacity to take up heat from the atmosphere.

The UN's Projections Are Disproven

Next, the UN has unwisely repealed the Stefan-Boltzmann radiative-transfer equation, the fundamental astrophysical law that relates changes in radiant energy to changes in temperature. The entire debate is about exactly that matter. Yet in 1,600 pages the UN does not mention this crucial equation once. Result: the UN's "no-feedbacks" value of lambda is way too high. As an eminent physics professor pointed out to me recently, if the UN were correct, global surface temperature would now be 20F higher than it is.

It gets worse. The UN's computer models predict that in the tropics the rate of increase in temperature five miles above the surface will be three times the rate of increase down here. But 50 years of atmospheric measurement, first by balloon-borne radiosondes and then by satellites, show that the air above the tropics is not merely failing to warm at three times the surface rate: for 25 years it has been cooling. The absence of the tropical mid-troposphere "hot-spot" indicates that the computer models—expensive guesswork—on which the UN's rickety case is founded are, in a fundamental way, misunderstanding the way the atmosphere behaves.

The real problem of the 21st century will not be "global warming" but resource depletion, starting with oil.

On top of the "radiative forcings" from greenhouse gases, the UN says the mere fact of temperature change will cause more change still, through what it calls "feedbacks." The UN has hiked the feedback multiplier by more than 52 percent since its 1995 report, without quite saying why. [Israeli scholar Nir] Shaviv and [American researcher Joel] Schwartz calculate that the sum total of all feedbacks is either nil or very small, [researcher Frank J.] Wentz report[s] that the UN has missed out two-thirds of the cooling effect of evaporation in its assessment of the water-vapor feedback; [University of Alabama professor Roy] Spencer finds that the cloud albedo feedback, which the UN says is strongly positive, is in fact negative; [Finland writer Jarl R.] Ahlbeck says the CO_2 feedback has been enormously exaggerated.

No Scientific Consensus

I have mentioned a dozen scientific papers. I could have mentioned hundreds more that challenge the UN "consensus." There has never been and can never be a scientific consensus on climate change. [Meteorologist Edward] Lorenz, in the [1963] landmark climate paper that rounded chaos theory, stated and proved his famous theorem that the long-run revolution of mathematically chaotic objects like the climate cannot be predicted unless one knows the initial state of the object to a degree of precision that is in practice unattainable. Whenever you hear anyone recite the propaganda mantra

"The Science Is Settled," laugh at his redneck scientific illiteracy. The science can never be settled.

[Researcher Klaus-Martin] Schulte reviewed 539 papers on "global climate change" in the scientific journals. Only one paper mentioned that "global warming" might be catastrophic, and even that paper offered not a shred of evidence for the supposed apocalypse.

Bottom line: a recent peer-reviewed paper [by scientist Richard Lindzen] says all the UN's climate sensitivity estimates should be divided by three. We don't have a climate problem. The correct policy to deal with a non-problem is to have the courage to do nothing. Don't let your legislators in Hawaii waste time on this non-problem. The real problem of the 21st century will not be "global warming" but resource depletion, starting with oil. Let your lawmakers do some real work, and get to grips with that.

Global Warming Is a Myth

Walter Starck

Walter Starck is a scientist and one of the pioneers in the scientific investigation of coral reefs.

Climate change looks more and more like becoming a catastrophe we inflict upon ourselves in trying to avoid one we have only imagined. The theory of catastrophic global warming due to CO_2 [carbon dioxide] emissions rests on two fundamental elements. One is that CO_2 absorbs infrared radiation. The other is that interactive computer models of climate have been constructed to show increased warming with increased CO_2. However, a couple of dozen different climate models all produce differing results in accord with the assumptions and estimates they each incorporate.

While the absorption of infrared by CO_2 is undisputed, the amount of such heating on global climate is highly uncertain. There is good reason to think it has been greatly overestimated. The current understanding on which the climate models are based is very incomplete. As for the widely publicised catastrophic consequences of warming, these are not even predicted by the models but are only speculations regarding such warming.

A Lack of Verification

Complex interactive models can be constructed and adjusted to produce any desired result. Without verification they reflect only the ideas on which they are based. The famed mathematical physicist and father of cybernetics, John von Neumann, once said: "If you allow me four free parameters I can build a mathematical model that describes exactly everything

Walter Starck, "Global-Warming—Myth, Threat or Opportunity?" *National Observer–Australia and World Affairs*, vol. 77, winter 2008, p. 43–47. Copyright © 2008 Council for the National Interest. Reproduced by permission.

that an elephant can do. If you allow me a fifth free parameter, the model I build will forecast that the elephant will fly."

Those who claim a high degree of scientific certainty regarding global warming can only be woefully uninformed, overly impressed with themselves or less than honest. There are serious doubts and uncertainties about every aspect. The fundamental radiative physics involved in the complex and variable mix of gases and conditions that comprise the global atmosphere is far from clear. The distribution of heat through the myriad pathways of atmospheric and oceanic circulation is only poorly understood. The innumerable interactions and feedbacks involved in this immensely complex system have only barely begun to be recognised, much less understood well enough to be accurately modelled.

The claim that the threat of global warming is 90 per cent (or often 99 per cent) certain is simply a figure of speech reflecting the speaker's commitment to a belief. It has no mathematical basis.

Real World Evidence

In contrast to the virtual world of computer simulations, real world evidence presents a very different picture. To list but a few key facts:

- Hundreds of peer-reviewed scientific studies from all over the world indicate a Medieval Warm Period as warm or warmer than present temperatures. Recent warming is not unprecedented.

- Numerous studies of extreme weather incidences indicate that recent occurrences are also not unprecedented, nor even unusual.

- The tropical mid-tropospheric warming predicted by the models as a prominent signature of CO_2-induced global warming has not occurred. The models are wrong about the dominant area of warming.

- Most of the warming predicted by the models comes from increased relative humidity acting as a positive feedback to amplify CO_2-induced warming. This too has not occurred. The models are thus also wrong about the major source of warming.

- Contrary to greenhouse warming expectations, southern hemisphere trends have shown negligible warming.

- The global temperature trend has been flat for a decade despite increasing CO_2.

- Most important of all, global temperatures have declined markedly in both hemispheres over the past two years, with widespread record and near record lows.

The current cooling was unpredicted by any models. Although warming advocates have tried to dismiss it as only natural internal variability, they have previously strongly denied any such possibility in connection with warming. Even if one accepts some natural variability, widespread record cold clearly refutes the degree of warming that has been attributed to the Greenhouse (GH) effect. Moreover, such cooling is fully in accord with well-established correlations of temperatures and solar activity as well as the major multi-decadal shift in oceanic conditions known as the Pacific Decadal Oscillation which has just recently switched into its cool phase. However, if we accept these influences to explain current cooling, then we must also accept their likely responsibility for most or all of the preceding warming.

The claim that the threat of global warming is 90 per cent (or often 99 per cent) certain is simply a figure of speech reflecting the speaker's commitment to a belief. It has no mathematical basis, and should be seen as comparable to the 100 per cent certainty professed by religious devotees that theirs is the one true faith.

Although one might expect that evidence that a serious threat may not really exist would be greeted with hopeful interest by anyone professing concern about it, the opposite is true. That global warming is no longer just a theory, but has become a belief is reflected in the reaction to any suggestion of doubt. No matter how well founded and clearly presented, this provokes only anger and rejection, not interest, in believers. As contrary evidence mounts and climate cools, defence of the belief only becomes more desperate and the claimed threats are ratcheted up still further. One might be forgiven the impression that the threats are not so much feared as they are fervently being hoped for.

The Oil Supply

Meanwhile, however, the obsession with global warming has blinded us to a far more real and imminent danger. The oil supply on which our entire economy is based is not keeping up with increasing demand, and we are doing nothing effective in response. Consider just a few important facts:

- Production has already peaked and is in decline in some 50 nations.

- Despite major advances in exploration technology and effort, the rate of discovery of significant new reserves has steadily declined for several decades and is far below depletion rates.

- Exports are decreasing in most exporting nations as their own domestic demand increases.

- Refining capacity has not kept pace with demand, due to environmental restrictions and concerns over future supply of crude.

- Most existing refineries are designed for light sweet crude, the supply of which is rapidly declining.

- Future oil will increasingly be heavy sour crude which only a minority of existing refineries can use.

- The major oil-producing nations have no incentive for massive investment to increase production, accelerate depletion, reduce their earnings and end up with huge expensive infrastructure which would soon be surplus to dwindling supply.

The price increases over recent years are primarily the result of near static supply in the face of increasing demand. Ongoing growth in demand, shortages, significant further price rises and a dampening effect on the global economy are almost certain to continue for the foreseeable future. While speculation may have contributed to accelerating the increases, it cannot sustain them. Their persistence and ongoing rise indicate a firm basis in underlying tightness in supply. Further price increases will only cease when cost suppresses demand.

Is Biodiversity Loss a Major Concern?

Chapter Overview

Anup Shah

Anup Shah is the founder and editor of GlobalIssues.org, *a Web site that aims to highlight a wide range of interrelated global issues.*

It is feared that human activity is causing massive extinctions. . . . [The] *Environment News Service* (August 2, 1999) says that "The current extinction rate is now approaching 1,000 times the background rate and may climb to 10,000 times the background rate during the next century, if present trends continue. At this rate, one-third to two-thirds of all species of plants, animals, and other organisms would be lost during the second half of the next century, a loss that would easily equal those of past extinctions."

A huge report known as the Millennium Ecosystem Assessment, started in 2000, was released in March 2005. Amongst many warnings for humankind, it noted that there has been a substantial, and largely irreversible loss in the diversity of life on Earth, with some 10–30% of the mammal, bird and amphibian species currently threatened with extinction, all due to human actions.

A [2006] report from the World Wide Fund for Nature (WWF) confirms previous years' concerns, that

> Already resources are depleting, with the report showing that vertebrate species populations have declined by about one-third in the 33 years from 1970 to 2003. At the same time, humanity's Ecological Footprint—the demand people place upon the natural world—has increased to the point where the Earth is unable to keep up in the struggle to regenerate.

Anup Shah, "Loss of Biodiversity and Extinctions," *Global Issues*, November 19, 2006. Reproduced by permission.

Research of long term trends in the fossil record suggests that natural speed limits constrain how quickly biodiversity can rebound after waves of extinction. Hence, the rapid extinction rates mean that it could take a long time for nature to recover.

The Impact on Ecosystems

Consider [also] the following observations and conclusions from established experts and institutions summarized by Jaan Suurkula, M.D. and chairman of Physicians and Scientists for Responsible Application of Science and Technology (PSRAST), noting the impact that global warming will have on ecosystems and biodiversity:

> The world environmental situation is likely to be further aggravated by the increasingly rapid, large scale global extinction of species. It occurred in the 20th century at a rate that was a thousand times higher than the average rate during the preceding 65 million years. This is likely to destabilize various ecosystems including agricultural systems.
>
> ... In a slow extinction, various balancing mechanisms can develop. No one knows what will be the result of this extremely rapid extinction rate. What is known, for sure, is that the world ecological system has been kept in balance through a very complex and multifacetted interaction between a huge number of species. This rapid extinction is therefore likely to precipitate collapses of ecosystems at a global scale. This is predicted to create large-scale agricultural problems, threatening food supplies to hundreds of millions of people. This ecological prediction does not take into consideration the effects of global warming which will further aggravate the situation.
>
> Industrialized fishing has contributed importantly to mass extinction due to repeatedly failed attempts at limiting the fishing.

A new global study concludes that 90 percent of all large fishes have disappeared from the world's oceans in the past half century, the devastating result of industrial fishing. The study, which took 10 years to complete and was published in the international journal *Nature*, paints a grim picture of the Earth's current populations of such species as sharks, swordfish, tuna and marlin.

... The loss of predatory fishes is likely to cause multiple complex imbalances in marine ecology.

Another cause for extensive fish extinction is the destruction of coral reefs. This is caused by a combination of causes, including warming of oceans, damage from fishing tools and a harmful infection of coral organisms promoted by ocean pollution. It will take hundreds of thousands of years to restore what is now being destroyed in a few decades.

... According to the most comprehensive study done so far in this field, over a million species will be lost in the coming 50 years. The most important cause was found to be climate change.

... NOTE: The above presentation encompasses only the most important and burning global environmental problems. There are several additional ones, especially in the field of chemical pollution that contribute to harm the environment or upset the ecological balance.

At the current rate of loss, it is feared the oceans may never recover.

Additionally, as reported by UC [University of California] Berkeley, using DNA comparisons, scientists have discovered what they have termed as an "evolutionary concept called parallelism, a situation where two organisms independently come up with the same adaptation to a particular environment." This has an additional ramification when it comes to protecting biodiversity and endangered species. This is because in the past what we may have considered to be one species could actually be many. But, as pointed out by scientists, by putting them all in one group, it under-represents biodiversity, and these different evolutionarily species would not [end] up getting the protection otherwise needed. . . .

Dwindling Fish Stocks

Mass extinctions of marine life due to industrialized fishing has been a concern for many years. Yet, it rarely makes mainstream headlines. However, a report warning of marine species loss becoming a threat to the entire global fishing industry did gain media attention.

A research article in the journal, *Science*, warned commercial fish and seafood species may all crash by 2048.

> *With massive species loss, . . . at* current *rates, in less than 50 years, the ecosystems could reach the point of no return, where they would not be able to regenerate.*

At the current rate of loss, it is feared the oceans may never recover. Extensive coastal pollution, climate change, over-fishing and the enormously wasteful practice of deep-sea trawling are all contributing to the problem, as *Inter Press Service* (IPS) summarized.

As also explained on this [GlobalIssues.org] site's biodiversity importance section, ecosystems are incredibly productive and efficient—when there is sufficient biodiversity. Each form of life works together with the surrounding environment to help recycle waste, maintain the ecosystem, and provide services that others—including humans—use and benefit from.

For example, as Steve Palumbi of Stanford University noted, the ocean ecosystems can

- Take sewage and recycle it into nutrients;

- Scrub toxins out of the water;

- Produce food for many species, including humans

- Turn carbon dioxide into food and oxygen.

With massive species loss, the report warns, at *current* rates, in less than 50 years, the ecosystems could reach the point of no return, where they would not be able to regenerate themselves.

While things look dire, there are solutions and . . . biodiversity can be restored quickly.

Dr. Boris Worm, one of the paper's authors, and a world leader in ocean research, commented that:

Whether we looked at tide pools or studies over the entire world's ocean, we saw the same picture emerging. In losing species we lose the productivity and stability of entire ecosystems. I was shocked and disturbed by how consistent these trends are—beyond anything we suspected.

The forests of the world have been exploited to the point of crisis.

"Current" is an important word, implying that while things look dire, there are solutions and it is not too late yet. The above report and the *IPS* article noted that protected areas show that biodiveristy can be restored quickly. Unfortunately, "less than 1% of the global ocean is effectively protected right now" and "where [recovery has been observed] we see immediate economic benefits," says Dr. Worm. Time is therefore of the essence.

Loss of Forests Equates to a Loss of Many Species

A 20-year study has shown that deforestation and introduction of non-native species has led about 12.5% of the world's plant species to become critically rare. (In fact, as an example, a study suggests that the Amazon damage is worse than previously thought, due to previously undetected types of selective logging and deforestation.)

A report from the World Commission on Forests and Sustainable Development suggests that the forests of the world have been exploited to the point of crisis and that major changes in global forest management strategies would be needed to avoid the devastation.

What also makes this a problem is that many of the endangered species are only found in small areas of land, often within the borders of a single country. New species of animals and plants are still being discovered. In Papua New Guinea, 44 new species of animals were discovered recently in the forests. Logging may affect these animals' habitats, though. The loss of rainforests around the world, where many species of life are found will mean that potential knowledge, whether medicinal, sustenance sources, or evolutionary and scientific information etc. could be lost. Brazil which is estimated to have around 55,000 species of flora, amounting to some 22% of the world's total and India for example, which has about 46,000 [flora] and some 81,000 animal species (amounting to some 8% of the world's biodiversity), are also under various pressures, from corporate globalization, deforestation, etc. So too are many other biodiverse regions, such as Indonesia, parts of Africa, and other tropical regions. . . .

The Misuse of Land and Resources

How land is used to produce food can have enormous impacts on the environment and its sustainability. And this often has nothing to do with populations. . . . [Indian scientist Vandana Shiva explains:]

> Junk-food chains, including KFC and Pizza Hut, are under attack from major environmental groups in the United States and other developed countries because of their environmen-

tal impact. Intensive breeding of livestock and poultry for such restaurants leads to deforestation, land degradation, and contamination of water sources and other natural resources. For every pound of red meat, poultry, eggs, and milk produced, farm fields lose about five pounds of irreplaceable top soil. The water necessary for meat breeding comes to about 190 gallons per animal per day, or ten times what a normal Indian family is supposed to use in one day, if it gets water at all.

... Overall, animal farms use nearly 40 percent of the world's total grain production. In the United States, nearly 70 percent of grain production is fed to livestock.

... In Indian Agriculture, women use up to 150 different species of plants (which the biotech industry would call weeds) as medicine, food, or fodder. For the poorest, this biodiversity is the most important resource for survival. . . . What is a weed for Monsanto [a major pesticide manufacturer] is a medicinal plant or food for rural people.

Because industrial agriculture promotes the use of monocultures, rather than a diversity of crops, the loss of biodiversity is leading to more resource usage, as described above. This as well as other political situations such as the motives for dumping surplus food on to developing countries to undersell the local farmers, leads to further hunger around the world. . . .

The Long Term Costs

If ecosystems deteriorate to an unsustainable level, then the problems resulting can be very expensive, economically, to reverse.

In Bangladesh and India, for example, logging of trees and forests means that the floods during the monsoon seasons can be very deadly. Similarly, many avalanches, and mud slides in many regions around the world that have claimed many lives, may have been made worse by the clearing of so many forests, which provide a natural barrier, that can take the brunt of such forces.

As the Centre for Science and Environment mentions, factors such as climate change and environmental degradation can impact regions more so, and make the impacts of severe weather systems even worse than they already are. As they further point out, for poor regions, such as Orissa in India, this is even more of a problem.

Vanishing coral reefs, forests and other ecosystems can all take their toll and even make the effects of some natural events even worse.

The cost of the effects together with the related problems that can arise (like disease, and other illness, or rebuilding and so on) is much more costly than the maintenance and sustainable development practices that could be used instead.

As an example, and assuming a somewhat alarmist scenario, if enough trees and forests and related ecosystems vanish or deteriorate sufficiently:

- Then the oxygen-producing benefits from such ecosystems is threatened.

- The atmosphere would suffer from more pollution.

- The cost to tackle this and the related illnesses, problems and other cascading effects would be enormous (as it can be assumed that industrial pollution could increase, with less natural ecosystems to "soak" it up).

- Furthermore, other species in that ecosystem that would depend on this would be further at risk as well, which would lead to a downward spiral for that ecosystem.

Compare those costs to taking precautionary measures such as protecting forests and promoting more sustainable forms of development. Of course, people will argue that these situations will not occur for whatever reasons. Only when it is too late can others say "told you so"—a perhaps very nasty Catch 22.

Many military forces of the world also have an effect on the environment.

Social costs to some segments of society can also be high. Take for example the various indigenous Indians of Latin America. Throughout the region, as aspects of corporate globalization spread, there is growing conflict between land and resources of the indigenous communities, and those required to meet globalization related needs. The following quote from a report [by environmental advocate Laura Carlsen] on this issue captures this quite well:

> Many of the natural resources found on Indian lands have become more valuable in the context of the modern global economy. Several factors have spurred renewed interest in natural resources on Indian lands in Latin America, among them the mobility of capital, ecological limits to growth in developed countries, lax environmental restrictions in underdeveloped nations, lower transportation costs, advances in biotechnology, cheap third world labor, and national privatization policies. Limits to logging in developed countries have led timber transnationals overseas. Increased demand and higher prices for minerals have generated the reopening of mines and the proliferation of small-scale mining operations. Rivers are coveted for their hydroelectric potential, and bioprospecting has put a price tag on biodiversity. Originally considered lands unsuitable for productive activities, the resources on Indian lands are currently the resources of the future.

> Indian land rights and decisionmaking authority regarding natural resource use on territories to which they hold claim threaten the mobility of capital and access to resources—key

elements of the transnational-led globalization model. Accordingly, increased globalization has generally sharpened national conservative opposition to indigenous rights in the Americas and elsewhere in the name of "making the world safe for investment." The World Trade Organization (WTO), free trade agreements, and transnational corporations are openly hostile to any legislation that might create barriers to investment or the unlimited exploitation of natural resources on Indian lands. The result has been a growing number of conflicts between indigenous communities and governments and transnational corporations over control of natural resources. . . .

The Military and the Environment

Many military forces of the world also have an effect on the environment. Sometimes, the scale of problems they leave when they move out of a training area or conflict is considerable. In some nations, such as the United States, the military can be exempt from many environmental regulations.

By no means a complete set of examples, the following illustrate some of the issues:

- In the Gulf War and Kosovo crisis, the US and UK [United Kingdom] used depleted Uranium which have environmental consequences as well.

- In the Vietnam war, the US used Agent Orange to defoliate the entire Vietnamese rainforest ecosystem. The effects are still being felt.

- In the Democratic Republic of Congo, various forces often kill gorillas and other animals as they encroach upon their land.

- In Okinawa, the large US military bases also affect the environment for the local population.

- [In] Vieques, Puerto Rico, the US use live rounds in bombing ranges, and low altitude flying for training. This also has had an effect on the environment.

Biocide Is a Bigger Threat than Global Warming

Rebecca Sato

Rebecca Sato has written for The Daily Galaxy, *an environmental Internet news site.*

Biocide is occurring at an alarming rate. Experts say that at least half of the world's current species will be completely gone by the end of the century. Wild plant-life is also disappearing. Most biologists say that we are in the midst of an anthropogenic mass extinction. Numerous scientific studies confirm that this phenomenon is real and happening right now. Should anyone really care? Will it impact individuals on a personal level? Scientists say, "Yes!"

A Colossal Threat

Critics argue that species disappear and new ones emerge all the time. That's true, if you're speaking in terms of millennia. Scientists acknowledge that species disappear at an estimated rate of one species per million per year, with new species replacing the lost ones at around the same rate. Recently humans have accelerated the extinction rate to where several entire species are annihilated every single day. The death toll artificially caused by humans is mind-boggling. Nature will take millions of years to repair what we destroy in just a few decades.

A recent analysis, published in the journal *Nature*, shows that it takes 10 million years before biological diversity even begins to approach what existed before a die-off. Over 10,000 scientists in the World Conservation Union have compiled data showing that currently 51 per cent of known reptiles, 52

Rebecca Sato, "Is Mass Species Extinction a Bigger Threat Than Global Warming?" *The Daily Galaxy*, February 6, 2009. Reproduced by permission.

per cent of known insects, and 73 per cent of known flowering plants are in danger along with many mammals, birds and amphibians. It is likely that some species will become extinct before they are even discovered, before any medicinal use or other important features can be assessed. The cliché movie plot where the cure for cancer is about to be annihilated is more real than anyone would like to imagine.

Research done by the American Museum of Natural History found that the vast majority of biologists believe that mass extinction poses a colossal threat to human existence, and is even more serious of an environmental problem than one of its contributors—global warming. The research also found that the average person woefully underestimates the dangers of mass extinction. Powerful industrial lobbies would like people to believe that we can survive while other species are quickly and quietly dying off. Irresponsible governments and businesses would have people believe that we don't need a healthy planet to survive—even while human cancer rates are tripling every decade.

A lot of us heard about the recent extinction of the Yangtze river dolphin. It was publicized because dolphins are cute and smart, and we like dolphins. We were sort of sad that we humans were single-handedly responsible for destroying the entire millions-of-years-old species in just a few years through rampant pollution. Unfortunately the real death toll is so much higher than we hear on the news. Only a few endangered "celebrity favorites" get any notice at all.

The causes of biocide are a hodge-podge of human environmental "poisons" which often work synergistically.

The Co-Extinction Phenomenon

Since animals and plants exist in symbiotic relationships to one another, extinction of one species is likely to cause "co-extinctions." Some species directly affect the health of hundreds of other species. There is always some kind of domino effect. This compounding process occurs with frightening speed. That makes rampant extinction similar to disease in the way that it spreads. Sooner or later—if gone unchecked—humans may catch it too.

Amphibians are a prime example at how tinkering with the environment can cause rapid animal death. For over 300 million years frogs, salamanders, newts and toads were hardy enough to precede and outlive the dinosaurs up until the present time. Now, within just two decades many amphibians are disappearing. Scientists are alarmed at how one seemingly robust species of amphibians will suddenly disappear within a few months.

The causes of biocide are a hodge-podge of human environmental "poisons" which often work synergistically, including a vast array of pollutants, pesticides, a thinning ozone layer which increases ultra-violet radiation, human induced climate change, habitat loss from agriculture and urban sprawl, invasions of exotic species introduced by humans, illegal and legal wildlife trade, light pollution, and man-made borders among other many other causes.

Is there a way out? The answer is yes and no. We'll never regain the lost biodiversity—at least not within a fathomable time period. . . . There are ways to prevent a worldwide bio collapse, but they all require immediate action. The eminent Harvard biologist Edward O. Wilson, and other scientists point out that the world needs international cooperation in order to sustain ecosystems, since nature is unaware of artificially drawn borders. Humans love to fence off space they've claimed as their own. Sadly, a border fence often has terrible ecological consequences. One fence between India and Pakistan cuts off bears and leopards from their feeding habitats, which is causing them to starve to death. Starvation leads to attacks on villagers, and more slaughtering of the animals.

Destructive Human Divisions

Some of the most endangered wildlife species live right in between the borderland area of the US and Mexico. These indigenous animals don't know that they now live between two countries. They were here long before the people came and nations divided, but they will not survive if we cut them off from their habitat. The Sky Islands is one of many areas smack in the middle of this boundary where some of North America's most threatened wildlife is found. Jaguars, bison, and wolves have to cross through international terrain in the course of their life's travels in order to survive. Unfortunately, illegal Mexican workers cross here too. People who know nothing of the wildlife's biological needs want to create a large fence to keep out Mexicans, regardless of the fact that a fence would devastate these already fragile animal populations.

Wilson says the time has come to start calling the "environmentalist view" the "real-world view." We can't ignore reality simply because it doesn't conform nicely within convenient boundaries and moneymaking strategies. What good will all of our money and conveniences do for us, if we collectively destroy the necessities of life?

There is hope, but it requires radical changes. Many organizations are lobbying for that change. One group trying to salvage ecosystems is called The Wildlands Project, a conservation group spearheading the drive to reconnect the remaining wildernesses. The immediate goal is to reconnect wild North America in four broad "mega-linkages." Within each mega-linkage, mosaics of public and private lands, which would provide safe migrations for wildlife, would connect core areas. Broad, vegetated overpasses would link wilderness areas normally split by roads. They will need cooperation from local landowners and government agencies.

It is a radical vision to many people, and the Wildlands Project expects that it will take at least 100 years to complete. Even so, projects like this, on a worldwide basis, may be humanity's best chance of saving what's left of the planets eco-system, and the human race along with it.

Human Health Depends on Plant and Animal Biodiversity

United Nations Development Programme

The United Nations Development Programme (UNDP) is the United Nations' global development network, which works to eliminate poverty around the world.

A new generation of antibiotics, new treatments for thinning bone disease and kidney failure, and new cancer treatments may all stand to be lost unless the world acts to reverse the present alarming rate of biodiversity loss a new landmark book says.

The natural world holds secrets to the development of new kinds of safer and more powerful pain-killers; treatments for a leading cause of blindness—macular degeneration—and possibly ways of re-growing lost tissues and organs by, for example, studying newts and salamanders.

But, the experts warn that we may lose many of the land and marine-based life forms of economic and medical interest before we can learn their secrets, or, in some cases, before we know they exist.

The new book, *Sustaining Life* [2008], is the most comprehensive treatment of this subject to date and fills a major gap in the arguments made to conserve nature.

A Promising Treatment for Peptic Ulcers Lost

A particularly illustrative example, highlighted by the book's authors [Eric Chivian and Aaron Bernstein], of what may be lost with species extinctions can be found in the southern gas-

United Nations Development Programme, "Newsroom: Biodiversity Loss—It Will Make You Sick," April 24, 2008. Reproduced by permission.

tric brooding frog (Rheobatrachus) which was discovered in undisturbed rainforests of Australia in the 1980s.

The frogs raise their young in the female's stomach where they would, in other animals, be digested by enzymes and acid.

Preliminary studies indicated that the baby frogs produced a substance, or perhaps a variety of substances, that inhibited acid and enzyme secretions and prevented the mother from emptying her stomach into her intestines while the young were developing.

The authors point out that the research on gastric brooding frogs could have led to new insights into preventing and treating human peptic ulcers which affect some 25 million people in the United States alone.

"But these studies could not be continued because both species of Rheobactrachus became extinct, and the valuable medical secrets they held are now gone forever," say Eric Chivian and Aaron Bernstein, the key authors of the book based at the Center for Health and the Global Environment, Harvard Medical School.

The findings, announced during the Business for the Environment Summit in Singapore, came in the run up to the 9th meeting of the parties to the UN [United Nations] Environment Programme (UNEP)-linked Convention on Biological Diversity (CBD) [which took place] in Bonn, Germany [in May 2008].

Here delegates from close to 190 countries; business leaders, academia and members of civil society [looked to] accelerate action to reduce the rate of loss of biodiversity by 2010.

Sustaining Life, the work of more than 100 experts and published by Oxford University Press, has been supported by UNEP; the Secretariat of the CBD; the UN Development Programme (UNDP) and IUCN [International Union for Conservation of Nature].

At the heart of the book is a chapter dedicated to exploring seven threatened groups of organisms valuable to medicine, including amphibians, bears, cone snails, sharks, nonhuman primates, gymnosperms, and horseshoe crabs that underscore what may be lost to human health when species go extinct.

Nearly one third of the approximately 6,000 known amphibian species are threatened with extinction. These animals produce a wide range of novel substances.

These losses include: promising new avenues of medical research and new treatments, pharmaceuticals and diagnostic tests.

Experts, including the authors, emphasize that the book's conclusions should not be construed as a licence to harvest wildlife in a way that puts further pressure on already threatened, vulnerable and endangered species.

Instead they should be a spur for even greater conservation and improved management of species and the ecosystems they inhabit.

Amphibians' Future Looks Bleak

The class Amphibians is made up of frogs, toads, newts, salamanders and caecilians—little-known legless organisms that resemble giant earthworms. Nearly one third of the approximately 6,000 known amphibian species are threatened with extinction.

These animals produce a wide range of novel substances, some of which are made only by amphibians living in the wild, not by those in captivity.

These include the:

- Pumiliotoxins, like those made by the Panamanian Poison Frog that may lead to medicines that strengthen the contractions of the heart and thus prove useful in treating heart disease.

- Alkaloids made by species like the Ecuadorian Poison Frog, which could be the source of a new and novel generation of pain-killers.

- Antibacterial compounds produced in the skin of frogs and toads such as the African Clawed Frog, and South and Central American leaf frogs.

- Bradykinins and maximakinins, made in the skin glands of species like the Chinese Large-Webbed Bell Toad, Mexican Leaf Frog, and North American Pickerel Frog that dilate the smooth muscle of blood vessels in mammals and therefore offer promising avenues for treating high blood pressure.

- Frog glue, produced by species such as the Australian frog, could lead to natural adhesives for repairing cartilage and other tissue tears in humans.

Nine species of bear are threatened with extinction including the polar bear, the Giant Panda, and the Asiatic Black Bear.

Many species of newts and salamanders, such as the Eastern Spotted Newt, can re-grow tissues such as heart muscle; nerve tissue in the spinal cord and even whole organs. As we are, in evolutionary terms, relatively closely related to these species, they are vital models for understanding how we might someday harness our own dormant regenerative potential.

Some frogs, such as the Gray Tree Frog and the Chorus Frog can survive long periods of freezing without suffering cell damage—understanding how these frogs do this may yield key insights into how we might better preserve scarce organs needed for transplant.

Bears Provide Fascinating Insights for Health and Medicine

Nine species of bear are threatened with extinction including the polar bear, the Giant Panda, and the Asiatic Black Bear.

The threats to bears are similar to those amphibians face, but in addition many bears are at risk because they are killed for body parts, such as gall bladders, which can command high prices in black markets in places like China, Japan and Thailand.

Several medical benefits have already arisen from the study of bears, including the development of ursodeoxycholic acid, found in the gall bladders of some bear species such as polar and black bears, into a medicine.

The substance is used to prevent the build up of bile during pregnancy; dissolve certain kinds of gallstones; and prolong the life of patients with a specific kind of liver disease, known as primary biliary cirrhosis, giving them more time to find a liver transplant.

Some bear species, known as "denning" bears because they enter into a largely dormant state when food is scarce, are of tremendous value to medicine as they are able to recycle a wide variety of their body's substances.

Unlike people, who if 'bed-ridden' for a five-month period can lose up to a third of their bone mass, bears actually lay down new bone during the denning period.

Several medical benefits have already arisen from the study of bears.

Bears appear to produce a substance that inhibits cells that break down bone and promote substances that encourage bone and cartilage-making cells. Currently, 740,000 deaths a year are the result of hip fractures worldwide, a large number of which are caused by osteoporosis.

By 2050 there will be an estimated six million osteoporosis-linked hip fractures globally.

Denning bears can survive for a period of five months or more without excreting their urinary wastes, whereas humans would die from the build up of these toxic substances after only a few days.

An estimated 1.5 million people worldwide are receiving treatment for end-stage renal disease, and more than 80,000 die each year in the U.S. alone from this disease. By studying denning bears, we may be able to learn how to treat them more effectively and help large numbers to survive.

Denning bears may also hold clues to treating Type 1 and Type II diabetes as well as obesity. Worldwide there are an estimated 150 to 200 million cases of Type II diabetes.

When produced in a non-invasive and ethically acceptable way, without pushing already threatened species further towards extinction, these substances are of great value to medicine.

Trees May Help Curb Alzheimer's, Epilepsy, and Depression

Close to 1,000 species of Gymnosperms [this classification includes pine and spruce trees] have been identified. Evolutionary, they are among the oldest of any plants alive, but many groups, such as the cycads, are classified as endangered.

Several pharmaceuticals, including decongestants and the anti-cancer drug taxol, have already been isolated from gymnosperms.

The researchers believe many more are yet to be discovered and may be lost if species of Gymnosperms become extinct.

Substances from one Gymnosperm, the Ginkgo tree may reduce the production of receptors in the human nervous system linked with memory loss. Thus they may play a role in countering Alzheimer's disease. They may also help in the treatment of epilepsy and depression.

Cone Snails' Habitats Are Threatened

Around 700 species make up the cone snails, seven of which were identified only since 2004. While only four are now classified as vulnerable, no thorough assessment has been made in over ten years, and thus current listings may underestimate the true number of endangered cone snail species.

For example, almost 70 per cent of some 380 cone snail species surveyed had more than half their geographic range within areas where coral reefs, their main habitats, are threatened.

There are at least 400 species of sharks . . . [but] many species are now threatened.

Cone snail species may produce as many as 70,000 to 140,000 peptide compounds, large numbers of which may have value as human medicines, yet only a few hundred have been characterized.

One compound, known as ziconotide, is thought to be 1,000 times more potent than morphine and has been shown in clinical trials to provide significant pain relief for advanced cancer and AIDS patients. Another cone snail compound has been shown in animal models to protect brain cells from death during times of inadequate blood flow.

It could prove a breakthrough therapy for people suffering head injuries and strokes and may even contribute to therapy for patients with Parkinson's and Alzheimer's. Other potential developments from cone snail peptides include treatments for urinary incontinence and cardiac arrhythmias.

Sharks Have Survived Millions of Years to Face Extinction Now

There are at least 400 species of sharks, which, as a group, evolved in ancient seas 400 to 450 million years ago.

Many species are now threatened, with some species, such as the Scalloped Hammerhead, White Shark, and Thresher Shark falling in numbers by as much as 75 percent over the past 15 years.

Over-fishing has been the main reason for the losses, and has been driven by an increased demand for shark meat as a substitute for traditional commercial fish catches in foods like fish and chips; the rise in consumption of shark fin soup; increases in by-catch, for example, in tuna fisheries; and an increased market for shark cartilage products for a variety of unproved medical purposes.

Squalamine, a substance isolated from sharks such as dogfish, especially abundant in their livers, may lead to a new generation of antibiotics as well as treatments against fungal and protozoan infections.

Studies are also being undertaken with squalamine compounds as possible antitumor and appetite-suppressant substances.

Trials are now also underway to see if squalamine can treat age-related macular degeneration which can lead to severe vision loss. The shark substance may halt the growth of new blood cells in the retina, which is linked to a loss of retinal function and blindness in these patients.

The salt glands of some sharks are also being studied to gain insight into how the human kidney functions and how chloride ions are transported across membranes, which may shed light on two diseases—cystic fibrosis and polycystic kidney disease.

Sharks, having evolved as some of the first creatures with a fully functioning 'adaptive' immune system are irreplaceable models to help us understand human immunity. "What potential these creatures may still hold to further our knowledge of immunity is being rapidly depleted with the mass slaughter of sharks and the endangerment of sharks worldwide," say the book's authors.

Several classes of peptides have been isolated from [horseshoe crabs'] blood that appear to kill a wide range of bacteria.

Horseshoe Crabs Have Become Fertilizer and Bait

There are four species of horseshoe crabs, with each organism possessing four eyes and six other light-detecting organs, as well as blood that turns cobalt blue when exposed to the air.

Because only around ten offspring survive out of the estimated 90,000 eggs produced by a female, they are highly sensitive to overfishing.

Once harvested and processed to be used as fertilizer, they are now used as bait for eel and whelk fisheries. Horseshoe crabs are also important in the food chain, especially for birds like the Red Knott, which rely upon the eggs for fuel over their 16,000 km migratory journey.

Horseshoe crabs also have tremendous value to medicine.

Several classes of peptides have been isolated from the creatures' blood that appear to kill a wide range of bacteria.

Another peptide from the horseshoe crab has been developed into a compound known as T140 which locks onto the receptor in humans that allows the Human Immunodeficiency Virus (HIV) to gain access into the body's immune cells. Preclinical trails indicate that the substance is at least as effective as the drug AZT at inhibiting the replication of HIV.

T140 has also shown promise in preventing the spread of certain cancers such as leukemia, prostate cancer and breast cancer, and as a possible treatment for rheumatoid arthritis.

Other cells in the blood of horseshoe crabs can, for example, detect the presence of key bacteria in the spinal fluid of people suspected of having cerebral meningitis. The test is so sensitive it can detect at levels of 1 picogram per milliliter of solution—roughly the equivalent of finding one grain of sugar in an Olympic-sized swimming pool.

[As] Achim Steiner, UN Under-Secretary General and UNEP Executive Director, [has] said: "Habitat loss, destruction and degradation of ecosystems, pollution, over-exploitation and climate change are among the powerful and persistent impacts that are running down the planet's nature-based capital, including the medical treasure trove of the world's biodiversity".

Marine Biodiversity Is at Great Risk

Nancy Knowlton

Nancy Knowlton is an adjunct professor of marine biology at Scripps Institution of Oceanography and is a renowned coral reef biologist.

News about ocean ecosystems is almost without exception grim. Collapsing fisheries, expanding dead zones, and the prospect of ever warmer and more acidic seas makes optimism a tough sell. When sounding the alarm bells, marine conservation scientists have focused primarily on the loss of "ecosystem services"—things like food, shoreline protection, and tourist-attracting seascapes—that translate into direct economic benefits for humankind. The fate of the basic building blocks of marine ecosystems, namely the many species that together make up the assemblages that provide those services, is far less often discussed.

This stands in contrast to the land, where worries about a sixth mass extinction associated with habitat destruction often underpin conservation concerns. To the public, mass extinction conjures up the demise of the dinosaurs due to a killer asteroid, but past cataclysms can be seen just as clearly in the records of marine species of clams, corals, crinoids, coccolithophores, and the like. These organisms may not grip the imagination like Tyrannosaurus rex, but their fossils tell us that things can go dreadfully wrong in the sea, with many once-dominant creatures vanishing in a geological instant. Scientists who study mass extinctions may disagree about causes in some cases, but they agree that such an event is not some-

Nancy Knowlton, "Marine Biodiversity in Jeopardy: The Attrition of the World's Coral Reefs Signals Far Broader and Graver Problems," *The American Prospect*, vol. 9, November 24, 2008, p. A15-16. Copyright © 2008 The American Prospect, Inc. All rights reserved. Reproduced with permission from The American Prospect, 11 Beacon Street, Suite 1120, Boston, MA 02108.

thing we want to initiate. In the most extreme case, the mass extinction that occurred at the end of the Permian Age about 250 million years ago, over 90 percent of all marine species went extinct. A repetition of an extinction event even remotely approaching this level would have consequences for humans that are so grave they defy imagination.

The Potential for Marine Extinctions

Why have marine conservation scientists focused so little of their attention on extinction? In part, this stems from earlier assumptions that marine species are more resilient than their terrestrial counterparts, thanks to their geographically broad distributions. We now know, however, that many marine species are much less widespread than we once imagined, as genetic studies have revealed sharp breaks between otherwise similar organisms living in slightly different habitats or on opposite sides of ocean basins. Thus, the potential of marine species to escape extinction by being in many places has probably been exaggerated. Nevertheless, it has been hard to imagine that humans could cause massive marine extinctions because of the vastness of the ocean, its inherent ability to buffer change, and the fact that people cannot populate its surface.

Even more worrying is the prospect of mass extinctions through wholesale degradation of marine environments, something once unimaginable but now all too real a prospect.

Indeed, the number of marine species known to have gone extinct globally is relatively small, in one analysis just 21. Some of these were spectacular large organisms, such as Steller's sea cow, the Caribbean monk seal, and the great auk, whereas others, such as most of the fishes, invertebrates, and seaweeds on the list, are known primarily to specialists. Interestingly, many of them went extinct not recently but before the first half of the last century. Not surprisingly, hunting was often the culprit.

Of course, the numbers of extinct species could soon grow, and grow exponentially. Catastrophic declines associated with fisheries have brought some species to the brink of extinction, either directly as targets or indirectly as bycatch. Leatherback turtles, the vaquita porpoise, and the white abalone are a few examples where only heroic efforts will suffice. It is worth noting that we do not have to directly kill every single member of a species to cause the species' extinction; rather, once a critical minimum population size is reached, the ability of the species to successfully reproduce can be lost, and its numbers inexorably decline. Marine species are also often difficult to breed. The vaquita, for example, are so shy that the only good photographs we have of them were taken after the porpoises were killed by drowning in fishers' nets.

Marine scientists no longer just talk about lost goods and services but also discuss permanent losses in the biological diversity of the planet.

Even more worrying is the prospect of mass extinctions through wholesale degradation of marine environments, something once unimaginable but now all too real a prospect. So many people live on or near the coast that almost all shallow waters have suffered, and even if some healthy habitat remains, extinctions can occur because the amount of suitable habitat available determines the number of species that can survive. Thus, some of the species that are still with us may in fact be doomed, a concept known as the extinction debt, which looms over the biosphere much as financial debt looms over the global economy.

The Threat of Global Warming

If humans affected only the shallow waters fringing our coast-lines, that would be bad enough. But thanks to greenhouse gas emissions, even the open oceans have seen and will continue to see increases in temperature and acidity. Both are bad because species often have rather narrow physiological limits, and the two changes together represent a kind of double jeopardy (triple jeopardy when you add in the fact that industrial fishing fleets go nearly everywhere and have stripped the oceans of most of its top predators). Often lost in the debate on climate change is the fact that carbon dioxide stays in the atmosphere for at least a century; even if we reform our ways instantly, extinctions are still likely to occur. Failure to take substantive action soon will bring large changes to the fundamental physical and chemical state of our oceans, something once thought impossible, and make the lessons of past mass extinctions increasingly and scarily relevant.

For these reasons, marine scientists no longer just talk about lost goods and services but also discuss permanent losses in the biological diversity of the planet, which we humans call Earth but whose surface is mostly ocean. Coral reef scientists have been among the first to raise the warnings, because they study the most diverse and arguably the most threatened of all marine ecosystems. Reefs today take up an area smaller than the size of Texas, and yet they house about one-quarter of all the species of the sea. Overfishing, pollution, invasive species, warming-caused bleaching, disease, and acidification have combined in perfect storm-like fashion to decimate reefs around the world. Living coral has declined by 80 percent in places like the Caribbean, and a recent study suggests that one-third of all corals are at risk of extinction. This is a level even higher than that estimated for frogs, once considered the most vulnerable of all life forms. Unlike frogs, however, corals create the three-dimensional structures, visible even from space, that shelter somewhere between 1 million and 9 million species. Reefs are indeed the canary in the oceanic coal mine, a canary that has passed out on the floor of its cage. Miners of the past paid close attention to their canaries, and so should we.

Biodiversity Loss Has Been Greatly Exaggerated

Sustainable Development Network

The Sustainable Development Network is a coalition of individuals and non-governmental organizations who believe in achieving sustainable development and environmental protection through efforts aimed at empowering people and developing and promoting policy discussions and solutions.

As commonly understood, biological diversity—or biodiversity—concerns all manner of living organisms on the earth, from microorganisms such as bacteria, to megafauna such as elephants, and of course, human beings. It is a complex web of ecological relationships and genetic variability (both in species and ecosystems). Biodiversity, then, is both local and global. It is by no means static, but constantly changing as organisms evolve and adapt.

A legalistic definition of biodiversity is "the variability among living organisms from all sources including, inter alia, terrestrial, marine and other aquatic ecosystems and the ecological complexes of which they are part; this includes diversity within species, between species and of ecosystems."

Biological diversity is a resource, valued, made use of, and augmented by human beings. These resources include forests, chemicals, fish, molds for antibiotics, and land conversion for agriculture, mining, and human residence. These resources are also augmented by conversion of land into wildlands, preservation of habitat, and through the use of new resources which in turn preserve others (replacing whale oil with petroleum, for instance).

Biodiversity Loss Is Exaggerated

The 'decline in biodiversity' has been greatly exaggerated. Between 1.4 and 1.6 million species have been named and described in the past three centuries. Estimates about the actual number of species on earth range from 5 million and 100 million species.

According to UK entomologist Nigel Stork, "only about 1,000 species are recorded as having become extinct in recent years (since 1600). If we know so little of the distribution and biology of most species, what then do we know of their 'threatened' status?"

The real extinction rate is probably close to 0.7 percent per 50 years.

[According to *The Skeptical Environmentalist*, a book by Bjorn Lomborg] "95 percent of the world's living species consist of beetles, ants, flies, microscopic worms and fungi, as well as bacteria, algae and viruses."

The claim of 40,000 species extinctions per year—that is, 10 to 100 percent of species over the next 50 years—is based on an assumption that 1 million species would become extinct in 25 years, with no data to support this claim. The source of this claim is *The Sinking Ark: A New Look at the Problem of Disappearing Species* (a book) . . . by Norman Myers.

Based on calculations by entomologists [Jonathan] Mawdsley and Nigel Stork, the real extinction rate is probably close to 0.7 percent per 50 years. This concurs with the United Nations Environment Programme's 1995 Global Biodiversity Assessment, which estimates that "the rate of extinction today is hundreds, if not thousands, of times higher than the natural background rate"—which equates to 0.1 to 1 percent per 50 years.

How to Use Biodiversity Sustainably

Price biodiversity. Specific species, genes, populations are already cultivated, and/or owned because of their economic value. But in the abstract, 'biodiversity' does not have any economic value, so no one knows how much or little biodiversity is wanted by people in the world. While not perfect, free economic exchange and property rights (see below) are preferable to the non-existent mechanisms for valuing biodiversity which exist today. Moreover, if the products of biodiversity are allowed to be exchanged and sold, there will be more biodiversity in the world.

Free international trade. Free trade will increase wealth for all people in the world. By increasing the value of economic output, people will afford more environmental amenities and will place a higher value on conservation.

Eliminate harmful subsidies. Subsidies to many kinds of industries which rely on renewable resources—agriculture and fishing, for instance—are environmentally destructive and promote overuse and over-harvesting. Removal of such subsidies would promote truly sustainable uses of biological resources and ecosystems.

Along with habitat conservation, restoration of wild species will help to ensure the existence of biodiversity.

Conserve habitat. Because the major threat to biodiversity loss is destruction of habitat, one of the primary ways to maintain biodiversity is by empowering people—individuals, local communities, and companies—to own and conserve private habitat as well as individual species. According to analyst Indur Goklany, the most important factor contributing to the loss of biodiversity, and deforestation, is "the loss of habitat and land conversion to meet fundamental human needs for food, clothing, and shelter."

Ensure human wellbeing. Fulfilling the needs of human wellbeing for all of the world's people should be first and foremost priority, even if it means sacrificing biodiversity.

How to Protect Existing Biodiversity

Restore species. Although local extinction may occur, private conservation can ensure that species survive in other places. Along with habitat conservation, restoration of wild species will help to ensure the existence of biodiversity. Allowing ownership of species would greatly assist this process.

Promote and develop technology. Resource-saving technologies, which allow for fewer resources to be used to produce the same quantity of goods, will help to save natural biodiversity. The widespread use of agricultural biotechnology would also be of great assistance in preserving biodiversity, by alleviating pressure on wildlands currently being converted to agricultural land. Since 1961, it is estimated that 3,350 million hectares of habitat have been spared from the plow because of technological advances.

Use property rights and legal recourses. To give people an incentive to engage in biodiversity protection, they should have a stake in the outcome of the management of biodiversity resources. Property rights should be extended to fish, to forests, and to agricultural land. Organizations, indigenous people, businesses, individuals—all of these should have the ability to own and manage resources, for whatever purpose they desire. Governments, on the other hand, tend to mismanage resources and use them for political gain, and are subject to the prevailing political winds. Land tenure and the legal system of property rights, however, gives individuals control over resources and encourages a long-run view which could take better account of biodiversity.

Some Species Should Be Allowed to Become Extinct

Murray Whyte

Murray Whyte is a staff reporter for The Toronto Star, *a Canadian newspaper.*

Consider the Jefferson salamander. About average-finger length, its grey skin mottled with black. Amphibious, spawning in Southern Ontario's quickly vanishing woodland vernal pools. Prognosis: Dying.

Now, the urban raccoon. Plump and furry, not so adept at fishing as its rural cousins, perhaps, but expert at garbage-tipping. An adaptable squatter in buildings both abandoned and, as homeowners near High Park well know, occupied. Prognosis: Thriving.

The tiny Jefferson, its numbers dwindling to endangered status as swaths of suburbanization razed its habitat, has become, in recent years, something of a cause célèbre.

For conservationists, it's a potent metaphor for our disconnect with the natural world, the vast land transformation that human activity has wrought—and our ineffectual attempts to counterbalance it. The raccoon, on the other hand, not so much. To sum up the popular opinion, our ring-tailed co-urbanite is simply a pest.

Mart Gross offers a different take. "Racoons wouldn't be in the city if they didn't fill a valuable niche," says Gross, a senior professor of conservation biology at the University of Toronto. "They're an important part of the ecosystem, and deserve the same protection as any wild species."

And the embattled Jefferson? "Basically, it's triage for the living dead," says Gross, on U of T's downtown campus. "Wildlife management has gone down the tubes because everyone's obsessed with endangered species. (The Jefferson salamander) is no longer adapted to its environment. It survives because we breed it in labs. Then, what we try to re-introduce to the wild is a different beast anyway, because it's adapted to its surroundings in the lab.

"The issue isn't a biological one, it's an aesthetic one. And we think it's so important that we give it rights. To me, that's the new conservation biology: Recognizing truly what it is that is the human goal, with biodiversity, and recognizing this concept of organisms having intrinsic rights is no more than a philosophical concept that bears little weight."

Endangered species without habitat . . . are no longer relevant to the ecosystem.

In the largely Catholic world of conservation biology, the idea that a native, endangered species like the Jefferson could be trumped by a trash-grubbing raccoon is a godless notion, to be sure. But the movement is growing. To be clear: Gross is not advocating a slash-and-burn mentality in the planet's remaining wildernesses. What he is suggesting, though, is equally offensive to some: To drop the battles we can't win and start thinking about the war. If that means accepting an altered landscape as a new arena where a different kind of biodiversity might flourish, so be it.

In his realm, Gross's ideas could be regarded as blasphemous: That endangered species without habitat, such as the Jefferson, are no longer relevant to the ecosystem; that nonnative species that find a way to thrive in their new environment—for example, the brown goby in Lake Ontario, a Mediterranean stowaway fish with an appetite for another invader, the zebra mussel—are welcome additions; and, most importantly, that these retrofits, re-do's and manipulations of the biosphere are simply evolution in action.

"The first change in attitude one should have is to think of humans as part of the natural world," Gross says. "We aren't inflicted upon nature. We are part of nature. We're a selective force, like wolves on moose and deer."

Many of these ideas are radical, and Gross will have a serious test today [July 13, 2008], when he and a group of his students present their work at the annual meeting of the Society for Conservation Biology in Tennessee, the field's largest and most influential gathering. "Ninety per cent of them, if they heard what we were discussing, they'd want to stone us," Gross says.

David Aborn, the University of Tennessee biologist hosting the affair, expects some lively debate. "You need that radical who's not afraid to stick his neck out."

Some would trade "radical" for "offensive." Among those is Caroline Schultz, the executive director of Ontario Nature, one of the advocacy groups fighting to keep the Jefferson alive. "The argument that we've wrecked their habitat, so we should just let it go, is a very nihilistic viewpoint.

"Some ideas are very interesting in academic realms but have to be very carefully applied—if at all—in reality."

As recently as 2004, however, Gross was the very picture of the religious conservationist, working feverishly for the Committee on the Status of Endangered Wildlife in Canada. That year, he identified two distinct salmon populations in British Columbia that had dwindled to dangerously low numbers. In an emergency measure, he recommended to then-environment minister Stéphane Dion that they be given immediate protection under the Species at Risk Act.

The issue is larger than any one species. What we want is ecosystem health.

Dion was legally obligated to comply, but he refused. Sockeye as a whole were not endangered, he argued, and protecting these two tiny populations would close down the entire multi-million dollar fishery.

"It was historic, a real groundbreaker," recalls Gross. "It was the first time in history a government had allowed a species to go extinct. And I was stunned. I just couldn't believe they'd let it go down the toilet like that."

Gross worked for more than a year to rally support. "To us, this was anathema [a thing to be loathed]—'You've got to save all these little twigs of the tree, because that's biodiversity,'" he says. "But then, I started to realize the issue is larger than any one species. What we want is ecosystem health."

The holy notion of the unspoiled wilderness is too narrow to begin to describe Gross's hypothesis on what, exactly, "wild" means.

"Don't bother with the conservation textbooks!" implores a line from a presentation Gross gave in May to the Canadian Society for Ecology and Evolution. "Take the religion out of conservation biology. Recognize humans as natural."

Gross's ideas are starting to gain traction. "If you were to look at the roster of scientists for the major conservation (organizations), you would not find anyone who studied evolutionary processes," wrote Peter Kareiva, the chief scientist and director of research for The Nature Conservancy, one of the U.S.'s largest conservation non-profits.

Kareiva did a survey of conservation organizations' websites—the World Wildlife Fund, the Wildlife Conservation Society, his own—hunting for the word "evolution." He found no occurrences.

"It's striking how comfortable we are talking about 'historical conditions' and what was 'natural in the past,'" Kareiva wrote, "yet fail to realize the extent to which change is so relentless, and that 'historical conditions' must by definition always be historical (and not some goal for which to strive)."

Kareiva was ruminating on a presentation that Gross had given The Nature Conservancy, and found himself moved by his ideas. "Language matters," he continued. The absence of evolution revealed "a view of the world in which the inevitability of change has been overlooked. Species go extinct, new species arise, and species adapt. An evolutionary biologist asks what types of traits and organisms are selected in different environments, and how humans are changing the attributes of biodiversity. We have an opportunity to shape the future of biodiversity that we may miss if we obsess too much over 'preservation' of the past."

Attempts to rebuild endangered populations rarely end well . . . despite the sometimes-massive efforts to do so.

Schultz believes there's a better balance to be struck. "Some say we should be striving to restore the landscape to a pre-European state—even if it's impossible," she says. "That might be going too far. But surely there's a moral imperative to keep a species alive, even if it's not pragmatic. The ultimate goal is to get the species back to the point where it can thrive."

But Gross's point is neither moral nor pragmatic, he says. It's simply the path that hews closest to a contemporary—and accurate—notion of "natural."

That being the case, attempts to rebuild endangered populations rarely end well, he says, despite the sometimes-massive efforts to do so.

Take the Chinook salmon. A system of hydroelectric dams along the Columbia River (its native habitat) has pushed it to the brink. "We closed their niche," he says. "But we have endangered-species laws that say we can't let them go extinct. So we've got truckloads of salmon being driven around the dams to release them so they can spawn. It's hopeless, and it's totally artificial."

Meanwhile, in Chile, the Chinook are thriving. How? We put them there. They'd never make it themselves—warm equatorial waters would kill them—but in the cool waters of the southern Pacific, the Chinook, introduced as farmed fish, are roaming free by the thousands. By next year [2009], they're expected to round Tierra del Fuego and head up the Argentine coast.

Some biologists would chafe at the "unnatural" horror such a situation presents. But a growing movement is looking to accept the invaders, usually placed by human hand, as natural selection unto itself, one of Gross's ideas.

"For a long time, (non-native species) were regarded as vermin," says the University of Tennessee's Aborn. "But now that they're entrenched, it's up to us to adjust our thinking."

The ability to "shape the future of biodiversity" could well be missed if conservation biology chooses . . . to look backward.

What does this have to do with the Jefferson salamander, or the raccoon in your garbage can? Well, everything. In a nutshell, the planet is doing what it has always done: Changing. That we've played such a significant role in that is secondary to the fact that, as always, the planet will be more hospitable to some species than others. As Darwin would have said, let the strong—or best suited—survive.

"I would say habitat is not being lost so much as it's being lost to them," Gross says. "But it's also being reconverted for other species as part of our evolving ecosystem."

Gross would see that as an opportunity. The Catholic in his field would see it as an abomination. But as Kareiva wrote, the ability to "shape the future of biodiversity" could well be missed if conservation biology chooses, as it does in large part now, to look backward, not forth.

Species Preservation Must Be Balanced with Competing Human Needs

David Stirling

David Stirling is vice president of the Pacific Legal Foundation and author of the book Green Gone Wild—Elevating Nature Above Human Rights.

The U.S. Supreme Court [heard, in October 2008,] . . . a case that could define how we approach national security.

Whatever one thinks of the war on terror or U.S. military activities in Iraq and Afghanistan, most Americans feel strongly that our men and women in uniform should have the most advanced equipment, weaponry and protective gear and be thoroughly prepared through training and practice to protect our national security.

Environmentalist organizations, on the other hand, believe federal environmental laws trump national security and the American military personnel who provide it.

That's why they filed a lawsuit against the U.S. Navy to stop its sonar training exercises off the coast of Southern California. Why? Because they claim marine mammals like the beaked whale—listed as "threatened" under the Endangered Species Act—were harmed when the sonar waves move through the ocean.

Whale Safety vs. American Safety

But for more than 40 years, the Navy has conducted training exercises with mid-frequency active (MFA) sonar and no incidents of harm or large-scale whale-beachings attributable to the exercises have been recorded. The Navy even recently is-

David Stirling, "Security vs. Species Preservation," *The Washington Times*, October 5, 2008. Reproduced by permission.

sued a lengthy environmental assessment stating there were no documented incidents of harm, injury or death to marine mammals resulting from exposure to sonar in the Southern California training area.

What's more, the National Marine Fisheries Service, the federal agency responsible for protecting and preserving marine mammals under the Endangered Species Act [ESA] and related statutes, issued a Biological Opinion concluding that the Navy's use of sonar was not likely to jeopardize the continued existence of any listed species. Nevertheless, a federal district court restricted the Navy's use of sonar so severely as to negate the training value of the exercise. But this will only serve to hurt our national security efforts.

With the quiet-running diesel-electric submarines used by erratic and unfriendly nations operating in the western Pacific and Middle East, the Navy regards its training exercises as the only effective means to prepare its strike groups to detect submarines before they close within weapons range.

The Navy believes restrictions on the use of sonar impose unacceptable risks to the timely deployment of strike groups to the Middle East and to national security. And the president issued an exemption to "enable the Navy to train effectively and to certify . . . strike groups for deployment" in support of operational and combat activities "essential to national security."

The 1978 Supreme Court decision in TVA v. Hill *. . . declared Congress intended the [Endangered Species Act] to preserve plant and wildlife species "whatever the cost."*

Despite these clear statements of the importance of the sonar training exercises, the U.S. 9th Circuit Court of Appeals upheld the district court's restrictions on the use of sonar, declaring, "The armed forces must take precautionary measures to comply with the [environmental] law during its training."

It's this elevation of the environmental laws to thwart national security preparedness that caused the Supreme Court to take up the case, *Natural Resources Defense Council [NRDC] v. Donald C. Winter, Secretary of the Navy.*

Some of the better-known examples of this disturbing trend include . . . timber harvests stopped in the name of the northern spotted owl.

A Faulty Line of Thinking

Hopefully, the court will set aside the long-held notion within the federal judiciary that the Endangered Species Act is a super statute that trumps all other public considerations. This faulty line of thinking got its start in the 1978 Supreme Court decision [that halted the building of a dam] in *TVA [Tennessee Valley Authority] v. Hill* (the snail darter case) where it declared Congress intended the ESA to preserve plant and wildlife species "whatever the cost."

Since the court's unfortunate use of that imperious phrase, federal district and appellate courts have regularly elevated species preservation above all other socially beneficial public interests.

Some of the better-known examples of this disturbing trend include: drilling halted for domestic sources of oil and natural gas because of listed species; timber harvests stopped in the name of the northern spotted owl, causing overgrown forests to be threatened by catastrophic wildfire; shutting off passage of river water to households and farmers during drought conditions for the benefit of fish; stopping construction of hurricane barrier gates out of concern for shrimp and shell fish—gates that would have protected New Orleans from [Hurricane] Katrina's deadly storm surge.

In deciding *Winter v. NRDC,* the Supreme Court could do the country a great and long overdue service by correcting the general misunderstanding of the ESA's species-preservation bias that followed the court's language—"whatever the cost." Removal of that mandate would restore to trial court judges their traditional role of weighing and balancing the equities between species preservation and competing economic and social public benefits.

Of course, litigious environmentalist organizations like those that filed the suit would vehemently oppose such a reasonable outcome, so holding one's breath is not recommended.

Editor's Note: In November 2008, in *Winter v. NRDC,* the U.S. Supreme Court ruled in favor of the Navy, finding that U.S. security interests clearly outweighed the possibility of harm to marine creatures.

Chapter 4

What Steps Are Necessary to Better Protect the Environment?

Chapter Preface

The Kyoto Protocol, often called simply the Kyoto treaty, is the world's main attempt to tackle the problem of global warming. This agreement was negotiated in Kyoto, Japan, in December 1997 as an amendment to the United Nations Framework Convention on Climate Change, an international treaty on global warming. The central thrust of the Kyoto treaty was a commitment by 40 industrialized countries to reduce their greenhouse gas emissions—the cause of rising global temperatures, according to most scientists. Specifically, the Kyoto Protocol sought to limit the global emissions of six greenhouse gases—carbon dioxide, methane, nitrous oxide, sulfur hexafluoride, haloalkanes (HFCs), and perfluorocarbons (PFCs)—by 5.2 percent as compared with 1990 emissions during the five-year period of 2008–2012. Under the terms of the treaty each country was assigned a specific goal, with some countries facing much higher goals than others.

The Kyoto Protocol attempted to achieve emissions reductions through two main strategies. One is a "cap-and-trade" scheme that allows participating countries (and in some cases states or regions within those countries) to trade emissions credits. Under this program, a country that cannot meet its emissions goal is permitted to purchase or trade for credits from countries that are exceeding their goals. This system encourages global emissions cuts without regard to their origin. A second strategy used under Kyoto rules is the Clean Development Mechanism, in which countries having problems meeting their emissions goals can offset their excess emissions by financing emissions-reducing projects in developing countries. A similar program, called Joint Implementation is available to encourage emissions-reducing projects in Eastern Europe and countries that used to be part of the former Soviet Union.

The Kyoto treaty faced obstacles from the outset, however, and has not been able to stop the rising levels of greenhouse gases in the atmosphere. An early problem was that the United States—the single largest source of carbon emissions, responsible for about 25 percent of global greenhouse gases—refused to ratify the treaty. U.S. President Bill Clinton, as well as his successor George W. Bush, never submitted the treaty to the U.S. Senate for ratification because they objected to the treaty's failure to cover developing nations. Even China—believed at the time of the treaty signing to be the world's second-largest emitter of greenhouse gases—was not required to reduce emissions. U.S. policy makers argued that this defect in Kyoto would place U.S. companies at a disadvantage and harm the U.S. economy. Australia, also a major source of carbon emissions, rejected the treaty for similar reasons. Without the United States and Australia, Kyoto became a treaty that primarily targeted Canada, Japan, and the European Union.

Of the countries that did sign and agree to be covered by Kyoto, many are having trouble meeting the treaty emissions targets and some have largely abandoned their emissions goals. According to recent reports, combined emissions from all Kyoto signatory countries have actually risen since 1994. And emissions from developing countries, which were never required to meet emissions reduction targets, have grown even more. Some commentators say China now is the leading source of global greenhouse gas emissions. Meanwhile, scientific warnings about global warming have become increasingly more urgent, with some studies suggesting that without drastic steps in the near future, the world may be unable to prevent catastrophic climate changes.

Despite the flaws of the Kyoto treaty, most climate change experts see it as the only viable path to reducing the emissions that are generating global warming. Efforts to negotiate an extension to the Kyoto treaty began on the Indonesian island of Bali in December 2007. Negotiators in Bali agreed on a two-year negotiating "road map" designed to lead to a new global warming agreement. Among the ideas embraced in the Bali agreement were measures for the developed countries to speed up the development and transfer of clean energy technologies. In addition, richer countries were expected to help developing countries control their greenhouse gas emissions and protect their forests, which help to absorb carbon dioxide, one of the most damaging greenhouse gases.

The most difficult issues in negotiating a new treaty, however, involve just how much countries will be required to reduce their greenhouse gas emissions during the next treaty period. The Bali agreement states that deep cuts in global emissions will be required, and it commits both developed and developing nations to move toward more sustainable development. The most important questions, however, will be answered in future negotiations—including exactly which countries will be required to commit to binding targets for emissions reductions, and how deep those emissions reductions will have to be to have any significant effect on global warming.

Since the Bali meeting, the European Union and several individual European countries have committed to making significant emissions cuts whether a new treaty is agreed to or not, but other countries have been less forthcoming. In fact, for years, the lack of global progress on climate change has been widely attributed to the fact that the world's two biggest polluters—the United States and China—were not covered by Kyoto and were otherwise unwilling to commit to acting on climate change. An atmosphere of distrust prevailed, with each superpower refusing to make emissions cuts unless the other also committed to emissions targets.

Yet according to many observers, recent events may be creating an unprecedented opportunity for this deadlock to be broken. The election of President Barack Obama, and increasing concern about climate change among Chinese leaders, may help the two nations to work together. The first step toward forging a partnership between the United States and China was taken when U.S. Secretary of State Hillary Clinton visited China in February 2009. In meetings with Chinese President Hu Jintao and other top Chinese officials, Clinton invited China to join the United States in an ambitious effort to curb greenhouse gases.

Experts say improvements in U.S.–China relations and the negotiation of a new Kyoto treaty could go a long way toward slowing global warming and improving the global environment. The authors of the viewpoints in this chapter discuss Kyoto's methods and suggest many other steps that could be taken to better protect the environment.

The New U.S. President Must Undo the George W. Bush Administration's Environmental Policies

Emily Bazelon and Paul Sabin

Emily Bazelon is a senior editor at Slate, *and Paul Sabin is executive director of the nonprofit Environmental Leadership Program.*

President [George W.] Bush's environmental policies may [have been] . . . alarming, but they are nevertheless worthy of study. This administration has used every last hammer, wrench, and saw in the executive toolbox to pursue its ideas about how we should use energy, land, water, and other elements of nature. And so . . . the next president . . . will similarly need to deftly deploy every trick of agency rule-making, executive order, enforcement of existing laws, and cooperation with Congress to reverse the damage done by the Bush administration and to usher in a new order.

The Administration's Environmental Responsibilities

Climate change. This is the green elephant in the living room. The Bush administration squandered eight crucial years by stalling and blocking any concerted national action to slow global warming . . . Barack Obama favor[s] strong federal climate legislation. If none of the current climate change bills gets passed . . . , the new president must immediately propose a new law to slash greenhouse-gas emissions in the first State of the Union address and make its passage a . . . priority. The

Emily Bazelon and Paul Sabin, "The Environment: Refocusing on the Environmental Crisis," *Slate*, April 3, 2008. Copyright © 2008 Washingtonpost.Newsweek Interactive Co. LLC. Reprinted with permission.

fate of the planet—no exaggeration—potentially depends on the United States moving quickly from climate laggard to climate leader.

The new president should also use his . . . executive powers to shift national policy—no need to wait for Congress. The U.S. Supreme Court ruled last year [2007] that the Environmental Protection Agency [EPA] has the power to regulate carbon dioxide emissions under the Clean Air Act. The EPA has done little since then, and a new president can direct the agency to start writing rules to that effect immediately. Likewise, a new administration can get out of the way of the various states that have taken climate change policy into their own hands. Where the Bush administration blocked California's request to regulate greenhouse-gas emissions, a new president can embrace California's initiative and encourage the other states seeking to experiment with environmental regulation in their own backyards.

Over the past eight years, the Bush administration has systematically dismantled environmental protections. . . . A new administration should . . . reverse course.

On his . . . own, a new president can also spur international action to fight global warming. Appointing a high-profile climate czar—Al Gore might be available and willing—could jump-start international climate treaty negotiations. Heck, maybe the new president can even show up occasionally, too. Back at home, a new high-level interagency climate office could begin to coordinate the economic, security, and environmental dimensions of the climate crisis, which will be with us for generations.

Climate is big, but the new president has other work to do, too. Over the past eight years, the Bush administration has systematically dismantled environmental protections by easing enforcement, reinterpreting policies, and blocking the imposition of stricter standards. A new administration should use the same executive powers to reverse course. Here are some representative messes the new president can clean up using executive authority:

The new president should restore the safeguards in the process for granting new oil and drilling leases.

Bush Enabled Environmentally Destructive Policies

New source review. Changes to this program with a snoozer of a name reveal the Bush administration at its most enterprising. New source review is the government's means of propelling the cleanup of aged power plants and industrial facilities. In the late 1990s, according to this great overview by Bruce Barcott in the *New York Times Magazine*, the power companies were on the verge of being forced into making widespread improvements to their emissions controls, changes that would have cut dangerous sulfur dioxide and nitrogen oxide pollution. Then the Bush Department of Energy came along and spearheaded the charge to gut new source review, steamrolling Christine Todd Whitman, then-head of the Environmental Protection Agency, and the agency's director of enforcement, Eric Schaeffer, who resigned over the controversy. The new Bush administration rules allowed the utility companies to wriggle out of their fix: They got 10 years' reprieve for installing any new pollution-control equipment, and they could make significant changes to their plants and still claim they were doing "routine maintenance," thereby avoiding expensive pollution control upgrades. The next president should announce ... that it's time to reconsider these rules and to come up with standards that will hold power companies accountable for the muck they spew into the air.

Ozone standard. . . . The [Bush] administration announced that because of the president's "last minute intervention," as the *Washington Post* put it, the EPA would weaken the agency's new ozone limits. After setting a tighter standard for long-term exposure of forests and crops to ozone than for short-term human exposure, the EPA, under pressure from the Office of Management and Budget and the White House, scrapped the separate long-term standard. The proposed limits were already more lax than those recommended by the EPA's scientific advisers. The new president should reverse this order—and others like it—by following the recommendations of scientists mandated by law to set scientifically based standards that protect human health and ecosystems and agricultural crops.

Policies Have Ignored Scientific Advice

More power to the White House. Here's another technical rule change with broad implications, ripe for reconsideration. [In 2007], the White House increased its sway over government agencies by requiring each agency to select a political appointee to oversee new rule-making and the guidance provided to regulated industries. The new president should scrap this order outright. While analyzing the costs and benefits is essential to efficient regulation, the Bush change undermines agency professionals and leaves regulatory initiatives to the political whims of the White House.

The Bureau of Land Management. Under Bush, the Bureau of Land Management has opened large swaths of land in states like Wyoming, Colorado, Montana, and Oregon to oil and gas drilling, often ignoring scientists' concerns about the effects on wildlife habitat. In the Pinedale, Wyo., field office, an internal review leaked in 2006 stated that there was often "no evaluation, analysis or compiling" of all the data demonstrating the consequences of such drilling on the surrounding land and water. The new president should restore the safeguards in the process for granting new oil and drilling leases, so development doesn't needlessly trash the patches of landscape that still look like the Old West.

Public science. Politicians often try to control the release of information, but the Bush administration has truly taken meddling with the findings of government scientists to an entirely new level. From sex education to mercury contamination and climate projections, the administration has blocked, altered, and suppressed crucial data and conclusions it doesn't like. The next president needs to give scientific expertise the respect it deserves by reporting results honestly and supporting work that's rigorous even when it's not expedient. Or profitable. Whether or not that helps halt global warming or preserve the landscape, it's a change worth making.

The World Must Curtail Greenhouse Emissions Even Faster than Previously Thought

Robin McKie

Robin McKie is science editor of The Observer, *a British newspaper.*

Along one wall of Jim Hansen's wood-panelled office in upper Manhattan [New York City], the distinguished climatologist has pinned . . . photographs of his three grandchildren: Sophie, Connor and Jake. They are the only personal items on display in an office otherwise dominated by stacks of manila folders, bundles of papers and cardboard boxes filled with reports on climate variations and atmospheric measurements.

The director of NASA's Goddard Institute for Space Studies in New York is clearly a doting grandfather as well as an internationally revered climate scientist. Yet his pictures are more than mere expressions of familial love. They are reminders to the 67-year-old scientist of his duty to future generations, children whom he now believes are threatened by a global greenhouse catastrophe that is spiralling out of control because of soaring carbon dioxide emissions from industry and transport.

"I have been described as the grandfather of climate change. In fact, I am just a grandfather and I do not want my grandchildren to say that grandpa understood what was happening but didn't make it clear," Hansen said [in January 2009]. Hence his warning to Barack Obama, [the new] US president. . . . His four-year administration offers the world a last chance to get things right, Hansen said. If it fails, global disaster—melted sea caps, flooded cities, species extinctions and spreading deserts—awaits mankind.

"We cannot now afford to put off change any longer. We have to get on a new path within this new administration. We have only four years left for Obama to set an example to the rest of the world. America must take the lead."

Only a carbon tax . . . would succeed in the now-desperate task of stopping the rise of [greenhouse gas] emissions.

The Need for Drastic Immediate Change

After eight years of opposing moves to combat climate change, thanks to the policies of President George [W.] Bush, the US has given itself no time for manoeuvre, he said. Only drastic, immediate change can save the day and those changes proposed by Hansen—who appeared in Al Gore's *An Inconvenient Truth* and is a winner of the World Wildlife Fund's top conservation award—are certainly far-reaching. In particular, the idea of continuing with "cap-and-trade" schemes, which allow countries to trade allowances and permits for emitting carbon dioxide, must now be scrapped, he insisted. Such schemes, encouraged by the Kyoto climate treaty, were simply "weak tea" and did not work. "The United States did not sign Kyoto, yet its emissions are not that different from the countries that did sign it."

Thus plans to include carbon trading schemes in talks about future climate agreements were a desperate error, he said. "It's just greenwash. I would rather the forthcoming Copenhagen climate talks fail than we agree to a bad deal," Hansen said.

Only a carbon tax, agreed by the west and then imposed on the rest of the world through political pressure and trade tariffs, would succeed in the now-desperate task of stopping the rise of emissions, he argued. This tax would be imposed on oil corporations and gas companies and would specifically raise the prices of fuels across the globe, making their use less attractive. In addition, the mining of coal—by far the worst emitter of carbon dioxide—would be phased out entirely along with coal-burning power plants which he called factories of death.

"Coal is responsible for as much atmospheric carbon dioxide as other fossil fuels combined and it still has far greater reserves. We must stop using it." Instead, programmes for building wind, solar and other renewable energy plants should be given major boosts, along with research programmes for new generations of nuclear reactors.

Clear Evidence of Warming

Hansen's strident calls for action stem from his special view of our changing world. He and his staff monitor temperatures relayed to the institute—an anonymous brownstone near Columbia University—from thousands of sites around the world, including satellites and bases in Antarctica. These have revealed that our planet has gone through a 0.6C [degrees Celsius] rise in temperature since 1970, with the 10 hottest years having occurred between 1997 and 2008: unambiguous evidence, he believes, that Earth is beginning to overheat dangerously. . . .

However, Hansen revealed his findings for 2008 which show, surprisingly, that last year was the coolest this century, although still hot by standards of the 20th century. The finding will doubtless be seized on by climate change deniers, for whom Hansen is a particular hate figure, and used as "evidence" that global warming is a hoax.

However, deniers should show caution, Hansen insisted: most of the planet was exceptionally warm last year. Only a strong La Niña—a vast cooling of the Pacific that occurs every few years—brought down the average temperature. La Niña would not persist, he said. "Before the end of Obama's first term, we will be seeing new record temperatures. I can promise the president that."

Messages of Doom

Hansen's uncompromising views are, in some ways, unusual. Apart from his senior NASA post, he holds a professorship in environmental sciences at Columbia and dresses like a tweedy academic: green jumper with elbow pads, cords and check cotton shirt. Yet behind his unassuming, self-effacing manner, the former planetary scientist has shown surprising steel throughout his career. In 1988, he electrified a congressional hearing, on a particular hot, sticky day in June, when he announced he was "99% certain" that global warming was to blame for the weather and that the planet was now in peril from rising carbon dioxide emissions. His remarks, which made headlines across the US, pushed global warming on to news agendas for the first time.

Over the years, Hansen persisted with his warnings. Then, in 2005, he gave a talk at the American Geophysical Union in which he argued that the year was the warmest on record and that industrial carbon emissions were to blame. A furious White House phoned NASA and Hansen was banned from appearing in newspapers or on television or radio. It was a bungled attempt at censorship. Newspapers revealed that Hansen was being silenced and his story, along with his warnings about the climate, got global coverage.

Since then Hansen has continued his mission "to make clear" the dangers of climate change, sending a letter ... December [2008] from himself and his wife Anniek about the urgency of the planet's climatic peril to Barack and Michelle

Obama. "We decided to send it to both of them because we thought there may be a better chance she will think about this or have time for it. The difficulty of this problem [of global warming] is that its main impacts will be felt by our children and by our grandchildren. A mother tends to be concerned about such things."

The ice caps . . . are now melting at an alarming rate and threaten to increase sea levels . . . enough to inundate cities and fertile land around the globe.

Nor have his messages of imminent doom been restricted to US politicians. The heads of the governments of Britain, Germany, Japan and Australia have all received recent warnings from Hansen about their countries' behaviour. In each case, these nations' continued support for the burning of coal to generate electricity has horrified the climatologist. In Britain, he has condemned the government's plans to build a new coal plant at Kingsnorth, in Kent, for example, and even appeared in court as a defence witness for protesters who occupied the proposed new plant's site in 2007.

"On a per capita basis, Britain is responsible for more of the carbon dioxide now in the atmosphere than any other nation on Earth because it has been burning it from the dawn of the Industrial Revolution. America comes second and Germany third. The crucial point is that Britain could make a real difference if it said no to Kingsnorth. That decision would set an example to the rest of the world." These points were made clear in Hansen's letter to the prime minister, Gordon Brown, though he is still awaiting a reply.

Imminent Peril

As to the specific warnings he makes about climate change, these concentrate heavily on global warming's impact on the ice caps in Greenland and Antarctica. These are now melting at an alarming rate and threaten to increase sea levels by one or two metres over the century, enough to inundate cities and fertile land around the globe.

The issue was simple, said Hansen: would each annual increase of carbon dioxide to the atmosphere produce a simple proportional increase in temperature or would its heating start to accelerate?

Each added tonne of carbon will trigger greater rises in temperature as the years progress. The result will . . . devastate most of the world's major cities.

He firmly believes the latter. As the Arctic's sea-ice cover decreases, less and less sunlight will be reflected back into space. And as tundras heat up, more and more of their carbon dioxide and methane content will be released into the atmosphere. Thus each added tonne of carbon will trigger greater rises in temperature as the years progress. The result will be massive ice cap melting and sea-level rises of several metres: enough to devastate most of the world's major cities.

"I recently lunched with Martin Rees, president of the Royal Society, and proposed a joint programme to investigate this issue as a matter of urgency, in partnership with the US National Academy of Sciences, but nothing has come of the idea, it would seem," he said.

Hansen is used to such treatment, of course, just as the world of science has got used to the fact that he is as persistent as he is respected in his work and will continue to press his cause: a coal-power moratorium and an investigation of ice-cap melting.

The world was now in "imminent peril", he insisted, and nothing would quench his resolve in spreading the message. It is the debt he owes his grandchildren, after all.

Biodiversity Hotspots Must Be Protected

E.O. Wilson

E.O. Wilson is a professor at Harvard University who has written and lectured widely in fields ranging from sociobiology and evolutionary psychology to conservation biology.

The tragedy unfolding in our ignorance, in our preoccupation with strictly physical environments, is that human action is destroying countless species and even ecosystems before we even know they existed. Many of them are millions of years old; all of them are exquisitely adapted to some particular part of the environment. . . . If you save the living environment, that's the rest of life around us, and the full diversity of it, then you will automatically save the physical environment too. But if you save only the physical environment and ignore the living environment, you will ultimately lose both. . . .

The 21st century, I believe, is going to be noted as the century of the environment. The immediate future can be usefully conceived as a bottleneck, of still-rapid population growth and high per capita investment and consumption. Science and technology, combined with a lack of self-understanding and the Paleolithic obstinacy that led to our ruinous environmental practices, have brought us to where we are today. . . . You can remember it best by thinking of us as being a Star Wars civilization: We have Stone Age emotions, medieval institutions and God-like technology. That's the source of all of our problems.

Saving Biodiversity Hotspots

Now, science and technology—combined with foresight and moral courage, both based from a more enlightened ethic, an

E.O. Wilson, "Protect Biodiversity Hot Spots and the Rest Will Follow," *Science News*, December 20, 2008. Republished with permission of Science News, conveyed through Copyright Clearance Center, Inc.

educated one—has to see us through this bottleneck. . . . [We need to] identify the hot spots: Those are the areas that have the largest number of endangered species. The habitats in them are mostly endangered and have the largest number of endangered species that will go extinct if the habitat is allowed to be destroyed. . . .

Fifty percent of all the known species of vascular plants, and 42 percent of all the mammals, birds, reptiles and amphibians, are in those hot spots, which occupy about 4 percent of the land's surface. . . .

The technology to [save biodiversity hotspots] exists, the cost really isn't very high and the benefits are beyond calculation.

It's been estimated that that 4 percent or so can be preserved, taking care of the people who live in and around it, economically, [for one payment of] about 50 billion euros. . . . That is one part in 1,000 of the annual combined gross domestic products of the world's countries. Could we come up with one part in 1,000, to save upwards of half a percent of the endangered species living on the Earth's surface? That's the kind of political solution and economic solution which would be impressive. . . .

The central problem of the new century . . . and the one that's going to count big time, long-term, is how to raise the poor to a global quality of life while preserving as much of the natural world as possible. Both the poor and biological diversity are concentrated together in the developing countries. The solution to this problem has to flow from the recognition that both depend on the other. The poor . . . have little chance to improve their lives in a devastated environment. Conversely, the natural environment where most of the biodiversity hangs on cannot survive the press of land-hungry people who have nowhere else to go. . . .

This is a problem that can be solved; the resources to solve it exist. Those who control them have many reasons to achieve that goal (not least their own security): The payout in science products, benefits, would be enormous compared to the relatively small costs globally that are required. The technology to do this exists, the cost really isn't very high and the benefits are beyond calculation.

Market Incentives Can Solve Environmental Problems

Fred Krupp

Fred Krupp has been president of the Environmental Defense Fund, a national nonprofit organization that links science, economics, and law to solve environmental problems, since 1984. He was also a founding member of the United States Climate Action Partnership. He is the author, with Miriam Horn, of Earth: The Sequel—The Race to Reinvent Energy and Stop Global Warming.

Until I was almost 30 years old, all indications were that I would spend my life as a conventional environmental lawyer, "suing the bastards." . . .

I armed myself with a law degree so I could go back and right [environmental] wrongs. I interned at two of the top organizations litigating against chemical and pesticide makers: the Environmental Defense Fund (EDF) and the Natural Resources Defense Council (NRDC). I then founded the Connecticut Fund for the Environment, with the intention of hauling "bad guys"—which, at the time, meant just about all business leaders whose work affected the natural environment—into court.

Thinking Like an Economist

But along the way, I changed my tack, if not my goal; I became the green community's chief advocate for using economic incentives to solve environmental problems. The *Wall Street Journal* has cheered me on, crediting me with a "singular style that serves business and the environment well." The

Fred Krupp, "The Making of a Market-Minded Environmentalist," *Strategy+Business*, Summer 2008. Reproduced by permission.

New Republic is not so sure, labeling me "The Devil's Advocate: He'll work with the GOP [Republican party], oil men, obdurate polluters, and any other stock environmental bête noire open to sitting down and negotiating. And, unlike most environmentalists, he shares their reverence for the marketplace." . . .

When an opportunity arose in 1984 to serve as executive director of the Environmental Defense Fund, I took it. A big part of the appeal was that people at EDF were beginning to put market mechanisms into play. The head of our California office, Tom Graff, who has degrees from Harvard Law and the London School of Economics, had hired Zach Willey, the first Ph.D. economist ever to work full-time at an environmental organization. They were developing a system to make water rights transferable. Instead of building new dams on California's last wild rivers, irrigation districts could sell their excess water to Los Angeles and use the money to finance more efficient irrigation systems and increase agricultural yields. At the same time, EDF software engineer Dan Kirshner was developing a computer model that demonstrated that conservation was the cheapest way to meet California's projected electricity needs. An EDF staff attorney, David Roe, took a case before the regulators, and ultimately Pacific Gas & Electric (PG&E) was persuaded to cancel plans for 10 new power plants, which lowered utility rates and increased shareholder returns even as it spared the atmosphere all that pollution.

When I arrived at EDF, however, only a minority of the staff supported this approach. Most staffers still wanted us to evolve into an organization like NRDC, built around first-class litigators. But a few people, ultimately including me, saw setting tough performance standards while harnessing markets as a far more powerful way to inspire human ingenuity on behalf of the environment.

Evolving the Environmental Defense Fund

I thought about it like this: Government must set the boundaries of what's allowed, including pollution levels. Regulators must crack down on those who violate the rules. But if you just prescribe limits and brandish sticks, with no incentives for companies to go beyond compliance, you squander the creativity of people ready to invent better ways to conserve natural resources and clean up the water and air. Instead, we had a chance to reach deep into the economy and enlist all kinds of entrepreneurs; we could give businesspeople a reason to want to be part of the solution, even if they didn't like environmentalists. And if we could unleash all that imaginative energy, we would have a far more powerful force for change.

At first, I couldn't do much to advance those ideas. At that time, EDF had no money in the bank, an expense budget of US$3 million, and just $2.25 million in income. We struggled to meet payroll every two weeks, and I had to lay people off. But we worked hard on our finances, and after about six months, I was able to hire one new person: an economist and natural resources professor named Dan Dudek. I'll never forget that interview. Dan painted an amazing, brilliant, comprehensive vision of a robust market in pollution reductions and the legal regime needed to make it work. Instead of having government trying to figure out the best technology, which either missed the best approach entirely or froze in place technologies that were becoming obsolete, this regime would get everybody across the economy working to invent new ways to reduce pollution.

During our meeting, I wasn't sure if Dan was loony or the greatest visionary I had ever met. But I took a chance and hired him. Right away, he began working on a rudimentary trading mechanism for phasing out chlorofluorocarbons. The Montreal Protocol on Substances That Deplete the Ozone Layer, an international treaty incorporating that trading mechanism, was written and ratified during the next few years;

it would ultimately take effect in 1989. Meanwhile, to further develop the intellectual foundations for market-based environmentalism, we organized a conference with Richard Stewart, an environmental law professor then at Harvard, who was an enthusiastic and profound thinker on using markets for environmental goals.

Flexibility and Its Discontents

In November 1986, with our budget at about $5 million and all the confidence of youth, I wrote an op-ed in the *Wall Street Journal* announcing the arrival of a "third wave" of environmentalism. The first wave, I explained, had begun in the era of Theodore Roosevelt, with the goals of conserving wild lands and wildlife; the second, born with the publication of Rachel Carson's book *Silent Spring* in 1962, had focused on stopping pollution and the harm it was doing to human health and ecosystems. Both waves had accomplished enormously important work, but they had also stirred a political backlash against environmentalists. As a group, we were viewed as reflexive opponents to industry and as hostile to growth, a privileged elite indifferent to job creation.

We saw that a national emissions market in sulfur dioxide could create a large-scale demonstration model for a way to rein in the greenhouse gases that cause global warming.

This third wave, I promised, would be constructive ... with environmentalists shouldering the burden of helping to find flexible and effective solutions, rather than just blaming others for the problems. The op-ed ended with a brief reference to using "market-oriented incentives" to achieve "greater environmental and economic benefits at a lower social and economic cost."

Those few words would ultimately open many doors. On the day of publication, I got a call from C. Boyden Gray, then the counsel to Vice President George H.W. Bush. He told me how refreshing it was to hear an environmentalist talking about markets, and he asked me to come to the White House to meet with him. . . .

After Bush's inauguration in 1989, I called Gray and we met again. During the New Hampshire primary campaign, environmentalists had elevated acid rain as a critical issue. Fish and plants in the lakes and forests of the Northeast had begun to die at an alarming rate, and scientists had determined that sulfur dioxide pollution from power plants was the primary culprit. Bush had promised that he would do something to tackle the problem. Gray told me that the president was serious about fulfilling that pledge and promised that "if you guys can write up a market-based plan, I'll make sure the president considers it." At EDF, my colleagues and I were already concerned about global climate change. We saw that a national emissions market in sulfur dioxide could create a large-scale demonstration model for a way to rein in the greenhouse gases that cause global warming.

Many of our early critics have come to appreciate the value of market-based regulations, largely because the results have been spectacular, right from the beginning.

Emissions trading had already been the subject of intense legal skirmishing all the way to the Supreme Court, but those cases involved emissions trading without a cap, fostered by individual states striving to improve air quality. Now we were proposing a federal emissions trading system, with a declining national cap. Because the idea was so radical within the environmental community, we were nervous. And we did stir passions. Some thought we were giving corporations a way to "pay to pollute," that emissions trading would just shuffle around the same amount of pollution. The Bush administration did try to get us to sign off on a trading mechanism without the cap, which would have been exactly that kind of shell game. But we refused to support it, insisting on a cap with a 50 percent mandatory cut, and deeper cuts over time. Bush ultimately took a stronger position on this issue than Senate Democratic Majority Leader George Mitchell had taken just a few years earlier. I thought that was pretty incredible. . . .

Mobilizing the Entrepreneurs

In the end, our advocacy of markets lost the Environmental Defense Fund some supporters. It even cost us one of our biggest donors. But ultimately our nonpartisan, market-based approach has won us support. There's been a great hunger for flexible, effective solutions among people who want a clean environment but who have been put off by some environmental strategies. And the fact that we've been able to get results, mining approaches that mobilize entrepreneurs—rather than being in denial about the world we live in—appeals to many people.

Over time, many of our early critics have come to appreciate the value of market-based regulations, largely because the results have been spectacular, right from the beginning. A few weeks after passage of the sulfur dioxide cap and trade law, I was invited to lunch in the White House mess with other members of the President's Commission on Environmental Quality, including Mike Deland, the president's environmental advisor, and PG&E CEO [chief executive officer] Dick Clark. Deland asked the White House chef for a plate of freshly baked chocolate chip cookies. When they arrived, Clark said the only way to eat cookies was with milk, so we all raised our hands and got a glass of milk. It was as if everyone in the room, like me, had been earnest kids themselves once, and suddenly that part of us had come to the surface. There over cookies and milk in the White House mess, Clark turned to me with a confession. When he'd heard me explaining to the president why we needed a market in pollution credits, he'd thought I had "lost it." But now that the law was in place, he had a pile of new proposals, both from his own shop floor and from outside consultants, for how PG&E could profit by reducing sulfur more than the law required. Environmental protection was no longer just a money loser, he realized, but a potential profit center.

At that moment, my enthusiasm for market-based environmentalism grew 10-fold. Because here, in the real world, was empirical evidence that these ideas were as powerful as we'd dreamed. Under the old rules, every power plant had to have a scrubber, adding tens of millions of dollars to the cost of the facility, even if the engineers could cut emissions more efficiently a different way. Every company had to cut the same percentage, even if some plants could make reductions far more cheaply than others. And overall emissions continued to rise as new plants came on line. But once the cap and trade system was in place, we watched power plants cut sulfur far faster than the law required, and at a fraction of the cost that the industry's leaders, constrained by old-system thinking, had predicted. . . .

Markets and Global Warming

In 1992, at the Rio Earth Summit, we proposed applying this strategy to carbon emissions. But our proposal was roundly rejected; instead, the delegates decided that each nation would make its own plan to get back to 1990 levels by the year 2000. Our group knew this would be futile. We'd seen the Clean Water Act prescribe zero discharge into the nation's waterways and instruct every state and county to devise a plan. And it hadn't worked.

Soon after Rio, a philosophical war began within the Clinton administration: Would they champion the old command-and-control approach in the next international negotiations in

Buenos Aires and then in Kyoto? Would they propose a carbon tax? Or would they advocate cap and trade? It was a knockdown, bloody fight, in which the Environmental Defense Fund was closely involved as one of the advising groups. We must have written a hundred memos and had as many meetings before our view prevailed. We worked with Larry Summers at the Treasury Department; John Podesta, President Clinton's chief of staff; Katy McGinty, who ran the White House Council on Environmental Quality; Hazel O'Leary at the Department of Energy; and Under Secretary of State Tim Wirth. And, finally, Clinton decided that cap and trade was consistent with his own "third way" political philosophy.

A cap and trade system . . . isn't based purely on free markets or voluntary action. It requires mandatory cuts in pollution and a government-created market.

Thus we helped write the American proposal for the 1997 United Nations Framework Convention on Climate Change in Kyoto, Japan. The cap and trade proposal was central to the grand bargain that the U.S. forced the rest of the world to accept in return for its agreement with the Kyoto Protocol reductions. The Europeans were quite opposed at first: They wanted "policies and measures." The tension between our organization and the European environmental groups was substantial. But although Kyoto was flawed in significant respects—requiring no emission reductions from developing countries and not dealing with forests in a sensible way—we ultimately found common cause in the need for mandatory reductions and real enforcement. The great irony, of course, is that after the United States demanded cap and trade, President George W. Bush turned his back on Kyoto, leaving the Europeans with the American mechanism but no American participation.

The Europeans went ahead anyway, starting their trading system in 2005 to prepare for Kyoto's 2008 start. The initial experience was mixed: Permits were over-allocated on the basis of industry's self-reported emissions. Even so, money is beginning to move toward solutions. In September 2006, at a meeting of the Clinton Global Initiative (an international forum of leaders), I heard venture capitalist John Doerr, a partner at Kleiner Perkins Caufield & Byers, describe innovations he was seeing emerge in response to the new carbon market. Though the European pilot program was just starting up, the signal was being sent and people in the real world were beginning to act in response. I had believed in this approach for a decade and had seen how well it worked for acid rain, but the sense of possibility was now so strong that I decided to write my book, *Earth: The Sequel.* I saw the power in sharing stories of the kinds of pioneers who will remake our energy infrastructure and, in the process, become billionaires.

The United States and the rest of the world should opt for an effective market system, unleashing a cascade of capital to solve the climate problem.

There Are Alternatives to Cap and Trade

A cap and trade system, of course, isn't based purely on free markets or voluntary action. It requires mandatory cuts in pollution and a government-created market. And markets are not an appropriate solution for every environmental problem. For particularly toxic substances such as mercury, which concentrate close to where they are dispersed into the environment, you need prohibitions, period. But for substances like carbon dioxide that don't have local effects, can't be banned, and are harmful in quantity, creative solutions must be found to ensure that human aspirations and human needs are met. And you need to have mechanisms that drive costs down.

One alternative to cap and trade is a tax, but a tax doesn't set a legal limit. Instead it requires government to guess just how high to set the tax to achieve the necessary reductions—another kind of prescience in which success is unlikely. Nowhere in the world has a tax actually solved an air pollution problem. In this case, the risk in guessing wrong is that the planet will go past the dangerous tipping point where disaster becomes impossible to reverse.

The other alternative to cap and trade is having laws and regulations that micromanage exactly how corporations will achieve environmental results. Corporations have long been aware of the limits of hierarchical micromanagement and have been moving for some time toward lean management, which radically decentralizes authority, conferring it on employees at all levels, and rewards incremental contributions that together are transformative. It's reasonable to think that as government agencies, companies, and groups like the Environmental Defense Fund continue to work together, all of these groups will become leaner, and thus much more capable, in dealing with the complexities of reducing waste, toxins, and greenhouse gases.

Encouragingly, [U.S. president Barack Obama] strongly support[s] using cap and trade to rein in global warming pollution. The end game will play out in Washington, D.C., and in 2009 in Copenhagen (where the international treaty that will replace Kyoto will be negotiated). At the Environmental Defense Fund, we are more convinced than ever that the United States and the rest of the world should opt for an effective market system, unleashing a cascade of capital to solve the climate problem and providing a context for the lowest-cost solutions to emerge. The sooner that happens, the sooner the Keeling curve will show a downturn in the atmospheric levels of carbon dioxide—promising a safer future for the planet.

The Market Cannot Solve the Environmental Crisis

Tony Iltis

Tony Iltis is a journalist who writes for the Green Left Weekly, *a progressive newspaper published by the Democratic Socialist Party in Australia.*

The good news is that politicians and corporations are finally recognising that there is an environmental crisis. The bad news is that the "solutions" being promoted by the establishment define what is realistic for capitalism, so the "need" for big business to remain profitable sets the parameters of what is "possible".

Symptomatic of this is the preponderance of economists on panels set up to investigate environmental questions and look for solutions. Market mechanisms that have created the problems are being posited as the solution.

Problems with Market-Based Solutions

The problem with market-based solutions is that profitability, by definition, involves a large share of resources going to increase the obscene wealth of the corporate elite, rather than meeting human needs, including the need for a sustainable relationship with the planet we live on.

Neither is it just that there is structural contradiction between profit and efficient use of resources: the more resources that are used to satisfy a particular need, the more profit is made.

Even to the extent that various schemes, such as creating markets of tradeable carbon emissions or water use rights, can provide financial incentives for corporations or individuals to

Tony Iltis, "Why the Market Cannot Solve the Environment Crisis," *Green Left Online*, June 29, 2007. Reproduced by permission of Green Left Weekly, www.greenleft.org.au.

decrease their environmental footprint, such a piecemeal approach is inadequate given the enormity of the problem. Furthermore, market mechanisms create a situation whereby solutions to one environmental problem can exacerbate others.

One of the most obvious environmental problems in [Australia] is the increasing shortage of water. The . . . government's solution is to commission a $1.9 billion desalination plant for [the capital city of] Sydney, to be built by a private consortium headed by French multinational Veolla.

However, not only do desalination plants contribute to oceanic pollution by releasing a toxic brine, they are extremely energy expensive and thus big contributors to global warming.

To remove the threat of catastrophic climate change, an increase in carbon sinks, . . . alternative energy and the replacement of short-haul aviation . . . needs to happen simultaneously.

The greenhouse gas emissions of the Sydney plant will be equivalent to a quarter of a million more cars on the road. Yet global warming is a major cause of Australia's water shortage as well as the tendency towards extreme weather events. This means that when rain does come, increasingly it is in the context of floods and storm surges. . . .

A realistic response to the water crisis would involve rainwater tanks, grey water recycling and an end to irrigation-based export agriculture and the access of mining companies to unlimited water. . . .

A Realistic Approach

A far more realistic approach [to global warming] involves immediately changing the way energy is produced. This has to involve the large scale roll-out of renewable technologies, such as wind and tidal power, and the abolition of coal burning power stations and wholesale reorganisation of society to reduce energy use. . . .

The problem with such a scheme is that to remove the threat of catastrophic climate change, an increase in carbon sinks, the roll-out of alternative energy and the replacement of short-haul aviation with ground transport needs to happen simultaneously.

The magnitude of the environmental crisis demands major changes in society.

Beyond Zero Emissions, a grassroots climate activist network, is campaigning for a high-speed electric rail network to replace short-haul flights between Adelaide, Melbourne, Canberra, Sydney and Brisbane. This is a realistic response.

In Melbourne, grassroots groups such as Link Up Melbourne, . . . and the Socialist Alliance are campaigning for the city's public transport system to be taken back from private operators, such as Connex, and for a massive expansion of both the level of services and the network so that no-one in Melbourne is without access to the system.

As more than half of Australia's greenhouse gas emissions are from road transport and only 9% of trips in Melbourne are by public transport, this campaign represents another realistic approach to climate change.

The magnitude of the environmental crisis demands major changes in society. Whole industries need to disappear. Others must be created. Patterns of settlement need to change. To expect market mechanisms and the profit motive to achieve these changes is unrealistic.

The Economy Must Be Reshaped to Save the Earth

New Scientist

The New Scientist *is a weekly international magazine that covers new developments in science and technology.*

Consumption of resources is rising rapidly, biodiversity is plummeting and just about every measure shows humans affecting Earth on a vast scale. Most of us accept the need for a more sustainable way to live, by reducing carbon emissions, developing renewable technology and increasing energy efficiency.

But are these efforts to save the planet doomed? A growing band of experts are looking at figures like these and arguing that personal carbon virtue and collective environmentalism are futile as long as our economic system is built on the assumption of growth. The science tells us that if we are serious about saving Earth, we must reshape our economy.

The Growth Dogma

This, of course, is economic heresy. Growth to most economists is as essential as the air we breathe: it is, they claim, the only force capable of lifting the poor out of poverty, feeding the world's growing population, meeting the costs of rising public spending and stimulating technological development—not to mention funding increasingly expensive lifestyles. They see no limits to that growth, ever.

Green values have no chance against today's capitalism.

In [2008] it has become clear just how terrified governments are of anything that threatens growth, as they pour bil-

New Scientist, "Special Report: How Our Economy Is Killing the Earth," vol. 200, October 16, 2008, pp. 40–41. Copyright © 2008 Reed Elsevier Business Publishing, Ltd. Reproduced by permission.

lions of public money into a failing financial system. Amid the confusion, any challenge to the growth dogma needs to be looked at very carefully. This one is built on a long-standing question: how do we square Earth's finite resources with the fact that as the economy grows, the amount of natural resources needed to sustain that activity must grow too? It has taken all of human history for the economy to reach its current size. On current form it will take just two decades to double. . . .

New Scientist brings together key thinkers from politics, economics and philosophy who profoundly disagree with the growth dogma but agree with the scientists monitoring our fragile biosphere. The father of ecological economics, Herman Daly, explains why our economy is blind to the environmental costs of growth, while Tim Jackson, adviser to the UK [United Kingdom] government on sustainable development, crunches numbers to show that technological fixes won't compensate for the hair-raising speed at which the economy is expanding.

Gus Speth, one-time environment adviser to President Jimmy Carter, explains why after four decades working at the highest levels of US policy-making he believes green values have no chance against today's capitalism, followed by Susan George, a leading thinker of the political left, who argues that only a global government-led effort can shift the destructive course we are on.

For Andrew Simms, policy director of the London-based New Economics Foundation, it is crucial to demolish one of the main justifications for unbridled growth: that it can pull the poor out of poverty. And the broadcaster and activist David Suzuki explains how he inspires business leaders and politicians to change their thinking.

A Shift from Growth to Development

Just what a truly sustainable economy would look like is explored in "Life in a land without growth," when *New Scientist* uses Daly's blueprint to imagine life in a society that doesn't use up resources faster than the world can replace them. Expect tough decisions on wealth, tax, jobs and birth rates. But as Daly says, shifting from growth to development doesn't have to mean freezing in the dark under communist tyranny. Technological innovation would give us more and more from the resources we have, and as philosopher Kate Soper argues in "Nothing to fear from curbing growth," curbing our addiction to work and profits would in many ways improve our lives.

It is a vision John Stuart Mill, one of the founders of classical economics, would have approved of. In his *Principles of Political Economy*, published in 1848, he predicted that once the work of economic growth was done, a "stationary" economy would emerge in which we could focus on human improvement: "There would be as much scope as ever for all kinds of mental culture, and moral and social progress . . . for improving the art of living and much more likelihood of it being improved, when minds cease to be engrossed by the art of getting on."

Today's economists dismiss such ideas as naive and utopian, but with financial markets crashing, food prices spiralling, the world warming and peak oil approaching (or passed), they are becoming harder than ever to ignore.

The Current Economic Crisis Provides Opportunities to Create a Sustainable Global Economy

Jonathan Lash

Jonathan Lash is president of the World Resources Institute, an environmental think tank.

Much of the world's attention is fixed on the brutal effects of the global financial crisis. But sooner or later—sooner we hope—the global economy will rebound. Markets will recover, and stocks will rise. Nature, on the other hand, does not do bailouts. The effects of today's greenhouse gas emissions—like those of yesterday and tomorrow—will be permanent, at least in the timescales that we care about.

They are what will shape the lives and markets of tomorrow.

My view of sustainability is very simple: what can't be sustained won't be. It was impossible for real estate values to continue to rise much faster than economic growth. It had to end sometime . . . and it did. When the bubble burst, the consequences were severe.

The same lesson applies to the ecological sphere. We simply cannot continue changing the chemistry of the atmosphere, through rising greenhouse gas emissions, without inviting enormous consequences. We cannot continue to increase human use of fresh water at twice the rate of population growth. Not only are there are limits on available supplies, but in many places these are reduced by climate change and pollution. Nor can we continue to create coastal dead zones, in areas where hundreds of millions of people depend on fisheries, by releasing ever more nitrogen into the surface waters of the Earth.

It is essential that these [economic recovery] decisions incorporate the risks and opportunities presented by a carbon-and-resource constrained world.

Since these behaviours can't be sustained, they won't be. The key question is whether we choose a managed transition to sustainability, or wait until the bubble bursts. That choice will have a profound effect on tomorrow's markets.

The Way Forward

So what is the solution, the way forward?

Nations are making vast investments in stimulus packages as they seek to retool their economies and revive productivity. It doesn't make sense to retool twice. We need to build for, and invest in, the economy of tomorrow.

Economic recovery around the world will be driven by thousands of firms in each country making decisions about what products to make, what technologies to use, and who to hire. It is essential that these decisions incorporate the risks and opportunities presented by a carbon-and-resource constrained world. It is critical that they create jobs in building the products that will help improve lives with reduced impact on the Earth's resources.

The financial crisis has created an enormous opportunity for change. In the United States, the [Ronald] Reagan era, an era of unrestrained free markets, in which government was regarded, at best, as a necessary evil, seems to have ended. In its place, there's a demand for government to be a source of solutions and a partner in implementation, particularly in dealing with the consequences of an economy that for the most part does not value the ecosystem services that underlie our well-being.

Right now is the best opportunity I have seen in 30 years as an environmentalist to align economic, social and environmental goals. The United States Climate Action Partnership [USCAP], of which WRI [World Resources Institute] is a founding member, and whose 26 corporate members include General Electric, Duke Energy, DuPont and General Motors, last week [January 2009] renewed and strengthened its call for the U.S. Congress to adopt a mandatory national cap and trade system to reduce current U.S. greenhouse gas emissions by 80 percent by 2050. The linked economic and environmental crises could have divided USCAP's members, but instead it renewed their determination to find reasoned solutions to the climate problem.

Right now is the best opportunity ... in 30 years ... to align economic, social and environmental goals.

On Inauguration Day, President Barack Obama also called for a new era of responsibility. I can't imagine a more important place for us to reflect this call than in taking responsibility for the effects of our actions on the global environment. We have the technology to mitigate those effects, and to create a new economy.

We need to seize the moment.

Organizations to Contact

The editors have compiled the following list of organizations concerned with the issues debated in this book. The descriptions are derived from materials provided by the organizations. All have publications or information available for interested readers. The list was compiled on the date of publication of the present volume; names, addresses, and phone numbers may change. Be aware that many organizations take several weeks or longer to respond to inquiries, so allow as much time as possible.

American Council on Science and Health (ACSH)
1995 Broadway, Second Fl., New York, NY   10023-5860
(212) 362-7044 • fax: (212) 362-4919
e-mail: acsh@acsh.org
Web site: www.acsh.org

ACSH is a consumer education consortium concerned with environmental and health-related issues. The council publishes the quarterly *Priorities*, position papers such as *The World Food Crisis*, and numerous reports, including *The DDT Ban Turns 30—Millions Dead of Malaria Because of Ban, More Deaths Likely* and *The Public Health Implications of Polychlorinated Biphenyls (PCBs) in the Environment.*

Biodiversity Project
214 N. Henry St., Suite 201, Madison, WI   53703
(608) 250-9876 • fax: (608) 257-3513
e-mail: project@biodiverse.org
Web site: www.biodiversityproject.org

The Biodiversity Project was founded in 1995 by a group of grantmakers, scientists, and advocates. Its mission is to make people aware of the importance of biodiversity and, through public education and communications programs, empower them to take actions to protect nature. The group's Web site sells numerous publications.

Cato Institute

1000 Massachusetts Ave. NW, Washington, DC 20001-5403
(202) 842-0200 • fax: (202) 842-3490
e-mail: cato@cato.org
Web site: www.cato.org

The Cato Institute is a libertarian public policy research foundation that aims to limit the role of government and protect civil liberties. The institute believes environmental regulations are too stringent and is a critic of global warming predictions. Publications offered on the Web site include the bimonthly *Cato Policy Report*, the quarterly journal *Regulation*, and numerous books and papers. Recent publications include *Is the Sky Really Falling? A Review of Recent Global Warming Scare Stories* and *The Costs of Reducing Carbon Emissions: An Examination of Administration Forecasts*.

Competitive Enterprise Institute (CEI)

1899 L St. NW, 12th Fl., Washington, DC 20036
(202) 331-1010 • fax: (202) 331-0640
e-mail: info@cei.org
Web site: http://cei.org

CEI is a nonprofit public policy organization dedicated to the principles of free enterprise and limited government. The institute believes private incentives and property rights, rather than government regulations, are the best way to protect the environment. CEI's publications include the newsletter *Monthly Planet*, and a wealth of policy briefs, books, and articles. Recent publications include *Obama CO2 Emissions Plans Would Wreck Economy, Auto Industry* and *Global Warming: It Isn't a Hoax and It Isn't a Crisis*.

Environmental Justice Resource Center (EJRC)

223 James P. Brawley Dr., Atlanta, GA 30314
(404) 880-6911 • fax: (404) 880-6909
e-mail: ejr@cau.edu
Web site: www.ejrc.cau.edu

Formed in 1994 at Clark Atlanta University, the Environmental Justice Resource Center serves as a research, policy, and information clearinghouse on issues related to environmental justice, race and the environment, civil rights, locations of environmental hazardous industries, land use planning, transportation equity, and suburban sprawl. Center officials assist, support, train, and educate people of color with the goal of facilitating their inclusion into mainstream environmental decision making. The EJRC publishes newsletters, proceedings, reports, and books, and its Web site contains a long list of links to other environment and civil rights organizations.

Environmental Protection Agency (EPA)
Ariel Rios Bldg., 1200 Pennsylvania Ave. NW
Washington, DC   20460
(202) 272-0167
Web site: www.epa.gov

The EPA is the federal agency in charge of protecting the environment and controlling pollution. The agency works toward these goals by enacting and enforcing regulations, identifying and fining polluters, assisting businesses and local environmental agencies, and cleaning up polluted sites. The EPA Web site provides useful background information about various environmental issues, and the agency publishes periodic reports and the monthly newsletter *Go Green*, which provides environmental tips for homes, communities, and offices.

Evangelical Environmental Network (EEN)
1655 N. Fort Myer Dr., Suite 742, Arlington, VA   22209
(703) 248-2602
e-mail: een@creationcare.org
Web site: www.creationcare.org

Evangelical Environmental Network is an evangelical ministry whose stated purpose is to "declare the Lordship of Christ over all creation." Network members encourage the Christian community to work together for true biblical stewardship and protection of the Earth's environment. The organization's main publication is *Creation Care,* a magazine published four times a year, but the Web site also provides factsheets and other resources on climate change and other environmental topics.

Foundation for Clean Air Progress (FCAP)

1801 K St. NW, Suite 1000L, Washington, DC   20036
e-mail: info@cleanairprogress.org
Web site: www.cleanairprogress.org

The Foundation for Clean Air Progress is a nonprofit organization that believes the public is unaware of the progress that industry has made in reducing air pollution. The foundation assists various sectors of business and industry in providing information to the public about improving air quality trends. FCAP publishes reports and studies demonstrating that air pollution is on the decline, including *Breathing Easier About Energy—A Healthy Economy and Healthier Air* and *Study on Air Quality Trends, 1970–2015.*

Global Warming International Center (GWIC)

PO Box 50303, Palo Alto, CA   94303-0303
(630) 910-1551 • fax: (630) 910-1561
Web site: www.globalwarming.net

GWIC is an international body that provides information on global warming science and policy to industries and governmental and nongovernmental organizations. The center sponsors research supporting the understanding of global warming and ways to reduce the problem. It publishes the quarterly newsletter *World Resource Review,* and its Web site includes press releases and news reports about global warming.

Healthy Child Healthy World (HCHW)

12300 Wilshire Blvd., Suite 320, Los Angeles, CA   90025
(310) 820-2030 • fax: (310) 820-2070
Web site: www.healthychild.org

Healthy Child Healthy World is a national nonprofit organization dedicated to educating the public, specifically parents and caregivers, about environmental toxins that affect children's health. HCHW was formerly known as the Children's Health Environmental Coalition. HCHW's publications include *First Steps*, a monthly e-mail newsletter that updates parents on environmental toxins in households and communities.

Natural Resources Defense Council (NRDC)

40 W. 20th St., New York, NY   10011
(212) 727-2700 • fax: (212) 727-1773
e-mail: nrdcinfo@nrdc.org
Web site: www.nrdc.org

The Natural Resources Defense Council is a grassroots environmental action organization that uses legal strategies, advocacy, and science to protect the environment, its plants and animals, and the natural ecosystems on which all life depends. NRDC publishes the quarterly magazine *OnEarth* and hundreds of press releases, factsheets, and reports. Examples include *Safeguarding Our Oceans in a Warming World: Addressing Global Warming and Ocean Acidification* and *Wildlife Refuge: Why Trash an American Treasure for a Tiny Percentage of Our Oil Needs?*

Nature Conservancy

4245 N. Fairfax Dr., Suite 100, Arlington, VA   22203
(703) 841-5300 • fax: (703) 841-1283
Web site: www.nature.org

The Nature Conservancy is a leading conservation organization that works to protect ecologically important lands and waters around the globe. Its mission is to preserve the plants, animals and natural communities that make up the Earth's biodiversity. The Conservancy publishes the *Nature Conservancy* magazine, and its Web site contains numerous articles and publications on biodiversity issues.

Pew Center on Global Climate Change

2101 Wilson Blvd., Suite 550, Arlington, VA   22201
(703) 516-4146 • fax: (703) 841-1422
Web site: www.pewclimate.org

The Pew Center on Global Climate Change is a nonpartisan organization dedicated to educating the public and policy makers about the causes and potential consequences of global climate change and informing them of ways to reduce the emissions of greenhouse gases. The Center publishes an e-newsletter as well as numerous reports and fact sheets, including *The Causes of Climate Change* and *The Science Behind the Shrinking Arctic Ice Cap.*

Property and Environment Research Center (PERC)

2048 Analysis Dr., Suite A, Bozeman, MT 59718

(406) 587-9591

e-mail: perc@perc.org

Web site: www.perc.org

PERC is a nonprofit research and educational organization that seeks market-oriented solutions to environmental problems. The center holds a variety of conferences and provides environmental educational materials. It publishes the quarterly newsletter *PERC Reports*, as well as articles, op-eds, and policy papers—among them *Environmental Justice: Opportunities Through Markets* and *The Environment: Greener Than Thou.*

Sierra Club

85 Second St., Second Fl., San Francisco, CA 94105-3441

(415) 977-5500 • fax: (415) 977-5799

e-mail: information@sierraclub.org

Web site: www.sierraclub.org

The Sierra Club is a grassroots organization, with chapters in every state, that promotes the protection and conservation of natural resources. The organization maintains separate committees on air quality, global environment, and solid waste, among other environmental concerns, to help achieve its goals. It publishes books, fact sheets, the bimonthly magazine *Sierra*, and the *Planet* newsletter, which appears several times a year.

Union of Concerned Scientists (UCS)

2 Brattle Sq., Cambridge, MA   02238
(617) 547-5552 • fax: (617) 864-9405
e-mail: ucs@ucsusa.org
Web site: www.ucsusa.org

The Union of Concerned Scientists aims to advance responsible public policy in areas where science and technology play important roles. Its programs emphasize transportation reform, arms control, safe and renewable energy technologies, and sustainable agriculture. UCS publications include the twice-yearly magazine *Catalyst*, the quarterly newsletter *Earthwise*, and various informative reports such as *Global Warming Human Fingerprints* and *Importing Pollution: Coal's Threat to Climate Policy in the U.S. Northeast*.

World Wildlife Fund (WWF)

1250 Twenty-Fourth St. NW, PO Box 97180
Washington, DC   20090-7180
(202) 293-4800
Web site: www.worldwildlife.org

The World Wildlife Fund is a multinational nature conservation organization dedicated to preserving the diversity and abundance of life on Earth and the health of ecological systems. WWF's Web site is a great source of information on endangered species, biodiversity loss, and climate change, and it references numerous scientific reports, studies, articles, and other publications. Recent examples include *A Global Map of Human Impact on Marine Ecosystems* and *Your Climate, Your Future*.

Worldwatch Institute

1776 Massachusetts Ave. NW, Washington, DC   20036-1904
(202) 452-1999 • fax: (202) 296-7365
e-mail: worldwatch@worldwatch.org
Web site: www.worldwatch.org

Worldwatch Institute is a nonprofit public policy research organization dedicated to informing the public and policy makers about emerging global problems and trends and the complex links between the environment and the world economy. Its publications include *Vital Signs*, issued every year; the bimonthly magazine *World Watch*; the annual report series *State of the World*; and numerous policy reports and publications, including *Oceans in Peril* and *Low Carbon Energy*.

Bibliography

Books

Rachel Carson, Edward O. Wilson, and Linda Lear

Silent Spring. New York: Mariner Books, 2003.

Eric Chivian and Aaron Bernstein, eds.

Sustaining Life: How Human Health Depends on Biodiversity. New York: Oxford University Press, 2008.

Laurie David and Cambria Gordon

The Down-to-Earth Guide to Global Warming. New York: Orchard Books, 2007.

Joseph F. Dimento and Pamela M. Doughman

Climate Change: What It Means for Us, Our Children, and Our Grandchildren. Cambridge, MA: MIT Press, 2007.

Daniel C. Esty and Andrew S. Winston

Green to Gold: How Smart Companies Use Environmental Strategy to Innovate, Create Value, and Build Competitive Advantage. New Haven, CT: Yale University Press, 2006.

Thomas L. Friedman

Hot, Flat, and Crowded: Why We Need a Green Revolution—and How It Can Renew America. New York: Farrar, Straus and Giroux, 2008.

Al Gore   *An Inconvenient Truth: The Planetary
                            Emergency of Global Warming and
                            What We Can Do About It*. Emmaus,
                            PA: Rodale Press, 2006.

Christopher C.   *The Politically Incorrect Guide to
Horner   Global Warming and
                            Environmentalism*. Washington, D.C.:
                            Regnery Publishers, Inc., 2007.

Nicolas Hulot,   *One Planet: A Celebration of
Phillippe   Biodiversity*. New York: Harry N.
Bourseiller, Steve   Abrams, Inc., 2006.
Bloom, Gilles
Martin, and Cal
Vornberger

Van Jones   *The Green Collar Economy: How One
                            Solution Can Fix Our Two Biggest
                            Problems*. New York: HarperOne,
                            2008.

Bjorn Lomborg   *The Skeptical Environmentalist:
                            Measuring the Real State of the World*.
                            Cambridge, United Kingdom:
                            Cambridge University Press, 2001.

————   *Cool It: The Skeptical
                            Environmentalist's Guide to Global
                            Warming*. New York: Knopf, 2007.

Thomas E.   *Climate Change and Biodiversity*. New
Lovejoy and Lee   Haven, CT: Yale University Press,
Hannah, eds.   2006.

James Maclaurin   *What Is Biodiversity?*. Chicago:
and Kim Sterelny   University of Chicago Press, 2008.

William McDonough and Michael Braungart	*Cradle to Cradle: Remaking the Way We Make Things.* New York: North Point Press, 2002.
Fred Pearce	*When Rivers Run Dry: Water, the Defining Crisis of the Twenty-first Century.* Boston: Beacon Press, 2006.
———	*With Speed and Violence: Why Scientists Fear Tipping Points in Climate Change.* Boston: Beacon Press, 2007.
Louise Spilsbury	*Environment at Risk: The Effects of Pollution.* Chicago: Raintree, 2006.
Crissy Trask	*It's Easy Being Green: A Handbook for Earth-Friendly Living.* Layton, Utah: Gibbs Smith, 2006.
Jay H. Withgott and Scott R. Brennan	*Environment: The Science Behind the Stories.* New York: Prentice Hall, 2007.
David Zeigler	*Understanding Biodiversity.* Westport, CT: Praeger Publishers, 2007.

Periodicals

ABC News	"Humans Spur Worst Extinctions Since Dinosaurs," March 21, 2006.
Business Week	"Another Inconvenient Truth: Behind the Feel-Good Hype of Carbon Offsets, Some of the Deals Don't Deliver," March 26, 2007.

John Carey
"The Real Costs of Saving the Planet; Critics Say Limiting Carbon Emissions Could Cost Trillions. But a New Study Suggests the Costs Are Much Lower," *Business Week Online*, December 4, 2007.

Melissa Checker
"Carbon Offsets: More Harm Than Good?" *Counterpunch*, August 27, 2008.

Christopher Dickey and Tracy McNicoll
"Why It's Time for a 'Green New Deal,'" *Newsweek*, November 1, 2008.

Tom Engelhardt
"Is Economic Recovery Even Possible on a Planet Headed for Environmental Collapse?" *Tomdispatch.com*, February 17, 2009.

Sigmar Gabriel
"Biodiversity 'Fundamental' to Economics," *BBC News*, March 9, 2007.

The Guardian
"50 People Who Could Save the Planet," January 5, 2008.

Van Jones
"The Stimulus: A Down Payment on a Green Future," *The Huffington Post*, February 17, 2009.

Brad Knickerbocker
"Will Global Warming Cause War?" *Christian Science Monitor*, April 19, 2007.

Katharine Mieszkowski — "Score One for the Environment: On Nov. 4, the Tension Was Unbearable. Fortunately for Our Air, Water and Wildlife, Barack Obama Triumphed," *Salon*, December 31, 2008.

New Scientist — "Africa's Water Crisis Deepens," March 11, 2006, vol. 189, iss. 2542, p. 6.

Kenneth Noble — "Our Hand in the Future: What Can Be Done to Avert Mass Extinction on a Scale Not Seen Since the Age of the Dinosaurs," *For A Change*, April–May 2004, vol. 17, iss. 2, p. 7.

J.R. Pegg — "State of the World 2008: Environmental Woes Sow Seeds of Sustainability," *Environmental News Service*, January 10, 2008.

Andrew Revkin — "A Shift in the Global Warming Debate," *The New York Times*, April 6, 2008.

Mark Rice-Oxley — "Financial Crisis Threatens Climate-Change Momentum," *Christian Science Monitor*, November 13, 2008.

ScienceDaily — "Americans Consider Global Warming An Urgent Threat, According To Poll," October 4, 2007.

Gus Speth — "How Our Economy Is Killing the Earth," *New Scientist*, October 14, 2008.

Peter N. Spotts   "Time to Begin 'Adapting' to Climate Change?" *Christian Science Monitor*, February 13, 2007.

Brian Walsh   "Heroes of the Environment 2008," *TIME*, September 24, 2008.

Todd Wilkinson   "New US Office Takes Fresh Approach to Carbon," *Christian Science Monitor*, February 3, 2009.

Jennifer Winger   "An 'Unequivocal' Change: Monumental Report Leaves Little Doubt that Humans Have Hand in Climate Change," *Nature Conservancy*, Summer 2007, vol. 57, iss. 2, pp. 14–15.

Carin Zissis and Jayshree Bajoria   "China's Environmental Crisis," *Council on Foreign Relations*, August 7, 2008.

Index